Opera
Biographies

This is a volume in the
Arno Press collection

Opera Biographies

Advisory Editor
ANDREW FARKAS

Associate Editor
W.R. MORAN

See last pages of this volume
for complete list of titles

The
Glory Road

Lawrence Tibbett

With a Discography by W. R. Moran

ARNO PRESS
A New York Times Company
New York / 1977

Editorial Supervision: ANDREA HICKS

———◆———

Reprint Edition 1977 by Arno Press Inc.

Discography Copyright © 1977 by W. R. Moran

OPERA BIOGRAPHIES
ISBN for complete set: 0-405-09666-6
See last pages of this volume for titles.

Manufactured in the United States of America

———◆———

Library of Congress Cataloging in Publication Data

Tibbett, Lawrence, 1896–1960.
  The glory road.

  (Opera biographies)
  Reprint of the 1933 ed.
  1. Tibbett, Lawrence, 1896–1960. 2. Singers—
United States—Biography. I. Title.
ML420.T52A3 1977   782.1'092'4 [B]   76-29972
ISBN 0-405-09711-5

THE
GLORY ROAD

The
Glory Road

By

Lawrence Tibbett

———

PRIVATELY PRINTED

1933

PRINTED BY E. L. HILDRETH & COMPANY, INCORPORATED
BRATTLEBORO, VERMONT

I

ALONG THE GLORY ROAD

IT seems to me that I have been unusually fortunate in having in my short but turbulent and hilarious and hysterical life a great number of moments that gave me real cause for rejoicing.

There was the night at the Metropolitan Opera House in New York when I sang Ford to Scotti's Falstaff, and the next morning awoke to find, for the first time, reporters and photographers and news-reel men at my door. There was the recent première of *The Emperor Jones* and there was the first night of *The Rogue Song*, a motion picture which the forecasters had predicted would be a very sour can of colored film and which I guessed would be worse—but which proved to be pretty good, after all.

But none of those moments compare in importance to one in Los Angeles when I was twenty-five years old. This was the turning point in my life.

I was just another hammy singer and didn't know it. In five minutes Basil Ruysdael, huge, hearty, blunt, with a torrid vocabulary, changed my entire point of view toward music. He made an honest baritone out of me.

He taught me how to pronounce "wind"—the wind that blows.

Ruysdael, now a radio announcer, had been a successful basso at the Metropolitan Opera House and had come to Los Angeles to teach singing. He was engaged by the California Opera Company to play the bass lead in a production of *The Mikado*, and I went to the theater where he was appearing to find out if I couldn't get a job in the show.

I had been singing in movie theaters and in churches and thought I was something very high-class. In choir lofts when I sang a solo I threw back my head and sang with eyes half closed and fixed upon my music, which I held parallel to the floor, at shoulder height, with arms extended. I was oozing Culture, Elegance, and Art.

Ruysdael, I knew, was a fine artist. I was determined to show him that even in Los Angeles there was at least one singer who had a true appreciation of the classics.

For my tryout I sang a love song, in my most elegant manner. It was about the wafting of the south wind, the frisking lambs, and God's own out-of-doors. I expected that it would knock Ruysdael over, but when I finished and turned to look at him he was still in a perpendicular position. He stepped up to me, put his fists on his hips, fixed a cold eye upon me, and said, "Listen, fellow, what is this south 'wined' that seems to be blowing out here in California?"

"Why, why——" I was flabbergasted. "Wined? Why, you know—wind."

"Uh, huh. What kind of language is this you're talking? What's this 'ahn-da' and 'lahm' and 'lo-va' and 'kees' and 'Gawd'?"

"Well, er," I tried to explain. "You know how it is—when you sing you pronounce a little differently."

"Why?" he demanded bluntly.

"Well, if you don't know, Mr. Ruysdael," I said hopelessly, "a big Metropolitan star like you—if you don't know, I can't explain. It's just that in high-class singing you say 'ahn-da' instead of 'and,' and 'lahm' instead of 'lamb.' I never heard a singer say 'win-d.' It's always 'wined.'"

I shall not attempt to record here the volcanic comment that my statement inspired. Women fled from the theater, one hand over one ear. Men trembled. My knees were shaking.

Finally Ruysdael calmed down and almost crushed my shoulder in his huge hand.

"Look here, fellow," he said. "Singing is just speaking words to music. Try that song again. Sing it as you would tell me about it if we were sitting together at lunch—just speak the words on the tune."

[2]

It was the best singing advice I ever had. It had never occurred to me that the best singing is the most natural singing.

I tried again, and for the first time in my life sang "win-d" instead of "wined," and pronounced naturally "love" and "God" and "kiss." When I finished I felt as stimulated as though I had taken a cold shower. The sham and the strut that I had believed to be a necessary part of Cultured music were wiped right out of my technique. It was a tremendous relief to find out that it was all right for a singer to be himself.

"That's better," Ruysdael said, when I had finished. "You ought to be able to do Pish Tush. You have a very fine voice and I'd like to help you. But listen," he warned me, "if you ever go arty on me, I'll break your neck."

As far as I know, from that time until this, I have never gone arty. I have had a few bad moments, however, with music committees in one or two churches. It seems that it is more reverent when you mispronounce words.

I am indebted to many teachers and conductors and coaches, but Ruysdael's instruction was the most important of all because he caught me in the formative period when I was about to build pompous-singer habits that might have lasted the remainder of my life. Later, Frank La Forge was to give me the push that put me into the Metropolitan Opera Company. He sent me from third base to home. But Basil Ruysdael put me on first.

After *The Mikado*, I sang in *The Fortune Teller* with him, and in another operetta, the name of which just now escapes me—the one with the "Sympathy" waltz in it.

Ruysdael charged $10 an hour for lessons, but when he found I had no money he taught me for nothing. He was a rough teacher. One of his stunts was to steal up, when I was singing, and yell, "Loosen up!" and give me a clout on the back that would almost knock me to my knees. I'd have to keep on singing no matter what he did to me. He would grab my jaw and shake it from side to side and abuse me roundly if, under such manhandling, I missed a note. As I sang *On the Road to Mandalay* he would make me lie face down on the floor, roll over, get up, and climb on a chair and jump down—and all the time he would be jabbing me in the ribs with his fist and shouting, "Relax! Relax!"

Many years later, at the Bohemian Grove, near San Francisco, I sang a rôle that called for a dramatic baritone solo as I trudged up a steep hill in the redwoods, and the newspapers said it was a remarkable feat. In *Emperor Jones* I sing as I roll on the ground, which acrobatic performance has called forth high praise. If the critics think *that* is good, they should have seen me in Ruysdael's studio lying on my back with my arms outstretched and my feet in the air, singing *I Love You Truly* and getting a touch of Ruysdael's boot every time I tightened up!

I had believed that I had a small voice, but he opened it, giving me power through relaxation. As a golf player gets a longer drive with a relaxed swing, so did I obtain more volume when I didn't try so hard.

The late Joseph Dupuy, one of the best tenors in southern California, had been my first teacher and was of inestimable service and encouragement to me. He was the first musician to tell me that some day I would be a fine singer. That I didn't get even more out of Dupuy was probably my own fault. He was too kind to me and I was lazy. I didn't like to sing those nerve-racking exercises—staccatos, legatos, scales, and cadenzas—that drive honest citizens wild on a summer night when they have a young singer in their neighborhood. I'll work night and day on a tune that means something, but I loaf on the exercises.

I am thirty-six years old, and as I look back it seems that whatever success has come to me has been a result of good luck and generous and patient friends. I was lucky in being born with a good voice, but that alone wasn't enough to carry me through. Added to the voice, thank God, was a passionate love of music, and my enthusiasm, instead of waning with accomplishment, increased year by year. I would rather sing than do anything else on earth.

In this good world are many gracious persons who believe that a good voice is a thing to be cultivated and nourished and who, with sympathy almost unbelievable, over and over again put new strength into my backbone and by lending me money and giving me their services cleared away the jungle that so often blocked my path.

It would be a silly affectation for me to pretend that I let Nature and my friends do all the work. At times I crawled on bloody hands and knees toward my goal; I slaved, I sacrificed, I fought, and died a hundred deaths. But for that I deserve not one cheer. Hundreds of thousands of men have struggled harder than I to achieve an ambition and every one of them has suffered more than I—for I did not suffer at all. I had a magnificent time.

It was a sporting adventure, and I think I am the most fortunate man I ever heard of, because I am making a living by *singing!* Just *singing!*

I am still astonished at my good fortune, for the ghosts of my conservative ancestors tell me that people achieve happiness only through hard work and that hard work is something which nobody likes to do. I feel a little as though I were a shopgirl who had been given a job paying a great deal of money, and her only duties were to go to the movies and chew gum. There must be a trick somewhere.

I do not pretend to understand the psychology that causes people to be so very kind to youngsters who seem to be qualified to become good singers. Potentially great actors, artists, scientists, doctors, architects, writers, statesmen do not receive nearly as much practical encouragement as is given to a young singer. It is quite unfair. But, for singers, it is very pleasant.

The first time I was helped out of a tight place was at a Methodist Church social in Bakersfield, Calif. I was six years old and on the program to sing a soprano solo—*Jesus Wants Me for a Sunbeam.* I was to sing without accompaniment, for in those days when I sang I just went ahead and sang, disregarding pitch and tempo, and no pianist living could transpose fast enough to get his notes into step with mine.

I faced the vast audience of 35 or 40 people and instantly forgot the words and music.

My mother was sitting in the front row, only a few feet away. She leaned over and whispered a cue, but I was too frightened to understand. She tried again. I shook my head helplessly and tears came to my eyes. The audience began to snicker.

A bit angry and disgusted with her stupid son my mother leaned forward and said, hopelessly, "Well, try *The Star-Spangled Banner.*"

With new lift I burst out with "Oh-oh say, can you see-ee!" The audience rose, joined in the singing, and, when we all finished, applauded with the gusto that people seem to believe should reward even the worst singer of a patriotic song. My début was a great success, thanks to my mother and the Grand Old Flag.

Many times since then I have wished that I were back in the Bakersfield Methodist Church, where I could extricate myself from an embarrassing situation by a device as simple as the singing of *The Star-Spangled Banner.*

For instance, there was my first appearance in *The Jest* at the Metropolitan Opera House in the spring of 1926, my third season there. The first three performances had been sung by Madame Frances Alda, Titta Ruffo, and Beniamino Gigli. Gigli sang the part that John Barrymore created on the stage and Ruffo sang Lionel Barrymore's.

Ruffo went to South America and I was given his rôle. It was my first leading part at the Metropolitan and of enormous importance to me. My only success up to that time had been as Ford in *Falstaff*, and the feeling was getting around the Met. that I was a one-part singer—the most damning tag that can be put on a man. Once the powers-that-be get that idea into their heads, you're through.

This was a great acting rôle as well as a singing rôle—a ruthless, powerful, murdering, brutal, jealous lover was Neri—and I decided that here was my opportunity to deliver the dramatic goods.

Madame Alda was the wife of Gatti-Casazza (behind his back we call him "The General"), the Master of the Metropolitan. Madame Alda was a power, too, a very great power, indeed. She helped me tremendously when I was trying to get into the Metropolitan, but now we were no longer friends because I had decided to try concert work alone, instead of going on tour with her quartet.

I was just an American youngster thrown into a cast with great artists—one of them the wife of the great Gatti-Casazza—and according to all rules and regulations I should have been content just to go along for the ride and not to attempt any driving on my own part.

But I was young and headstrong and ambitious. My Neri tore furiously through back-stage tradition. The author had written me rough, and, believe me, I was rough—in spite of Alda's angry protests, hissed between arias.

She was playing the part of my faithless mistress and, according to the story, I was supposed to fly at her in a jealous rage. Momentarily living the part, I lost my head. I struggled with her and threw her from me—and, *kerplunk*, flat on her back in the middle of the stage, feet flying, lay the outraged form of Madame Gatti-Casazza! My boss's wife!

"Oof!" she said. That was all she said then, but what she said at the end of the act was plenty!

I apologized profusely. I was terrified. Perhaps this might mean the finish of everything for me!

That wasn't the end of my troubles. In the last act I was supposed to push her violently off-stage, through a door. In my nervousness I pushed her too soon, and a man who was standing off-stage, waiting to catch her, missed Madame Alda completely and down she went again!

After that all went black. I must have gone satisfactorily through the motions for the remainder of the opera, for the newspapers the next day were very kind. But after Madame Alda took her second sprawling fall I remembered nothing until a friend came into my dressing-room and found me staring blankly into the mirror.

"What do you think this is, Fourth of July?" he asked.

I had been singing *The Star-Spangled Banner*.

I was desolate. The betting was 10 to 1 that Madame Alda would have me thrown out of the Metropolitan Opera House in revenge for her outraged dignity and bruised upholstery. It didn't help a bit when I heard someone—I think it was Gigli—go past my dressing-room humming Chopin's *Funeral March*.

But, except for the fact that Madame Alda refused to speak to me, business continued as usual. Ordinary business, that is. The special acrobatic stage business that my too-realistic portrayal had injected into the production was omitted from then on.

A few months later the opera company was in Atlanta, Ga., and after a performance of *The Jest* a party was given for us. It was a gay party, toasts were drunk, and finally some Atlanta Sir Walter Raleigh proposed that in order to prove our tremendous admiration for Madame Alda, we men should all file past her and each reward her with a kiss. I found myself in line, not knowing just what would happen when it came my turn to kiss a lady who loathed me.

"Well," I said when I reached her, "this is just as embarrassing for me as it is for you. Shall we make up?"

"Of course," she laughed, and I kissed her.

I am a loyal native of southern California, but I must admit that the climate of Atlanta has its moments. If it could so warm and soften Alda's heart toward me, probably Al Capone will emerge from the Atlanta penitentiary a benign, tender, and forgiving citizen!

In Cleveland a few years later Maria Jeritza and I had a battle on the stage, somewhat similar to the one I had in *The Jest* with Alda— only this was no accident. We were giving *Tosca*, and I was singing Scarpia.

Jeritza had a trick of changing stage business to suit herself. In the last scene Scarpia attacks Tosca and she falls to the floor. From that position she sings her aria. That was the way we had rehearsed it. But this time Jeritza wanted to sing from the far side of the stage, where she would be alone in the spotlight.

As I held her, she whispered, "Let me go! Let me go!"

I hung on, at first not understanding. Before the act began she had said to me, "This is our last performance. Let's make it a good one. Let's go after each other!" So now when she pounded and pushed me I thought she was acting.

When I realized what she wanted to do, I stubbornly decided that there would be a dead Tibbett on the stage before she took over the entire scene for herself.

We fought like wildcats. Following the stage directions, I tried to kiss her on her shoulders. She lunged at me, and the sequins on her dress made deep cuts in my chin. I pulled her hair and she pulled mine. She just wouldn't fall. I wore a heavy brass chain around my neck and she yanked it and broke it, cutting the flesh as the links parted. Neither of us could sing. We just muttered and gasped. Both of us had lost our heads. Jeritza was determined that she would get to the other side of the stage. I made up my mind that she would sing at my feet. I managed to get a hold that was a mixture of hammer lock and half nelson, and I threw her on a couch. She gasped, rolled to the floor—and sang! I had won the wrestling match!

When the act ended we looked like a couple of stray cats. The applause was tremendous. We took our bows and I got ready to weather a volley of invective.

The audience was still applauding when we started toward our dressing-rooms. She looked at me, smoothed her hair, and smiled.

"Well," she said, "we gave them their money's worth."

You never can tell which way opera temperament is going to jump.

I think it was a subconscious spirit of revolt against any surrender to special privilege or knee-bending to monarchs that made me behave not at all like a polite, self-effacing gentleman in the scenes with Alda and Jeritza.

THE GLORY ROAD

When I was a kid in Manual Arts High School in Los Angeles, I discovered Karl Marx and Robert Ingersoll and Emma Goldman and Tolstoy, and tried to follow them all at one and the same time. Later my radicalism became diluted with common sense, but I am still a nonconformist.

I lost my first great crusade—because my high-school principal was a true diplomat.

I organized a revolt against neckties on hot days, and a dozen of us appeared in school with shirts open almost to our waists. The principal sent us home and told us not to come back until we were fully dressed. I stayed out for two days, determined to give up an education before I would surrender to convention. Then the principal sent for me. The other boys had dressed up and returned to school.

If the principal had used honest argument, if he had threatened dire consequences, I would have resisted until the end—or at least, until my mother took a militant hand in the proceedings. But he played a dirty trick on me. He just said, "With your scrawny neck, Tibbett, and your funny face, you look like a giraffe. Why don't you cover up that Adam's apple and try to look halfway like a human being?"

Humiliated, I went home and put on a tie.

Nothing, however, has been able to temper my radical ideas about music, for no one has ever convinced me that they are radical at all—they're just common sense. From the day I learned to pronounce "wind" and to sing "have" instead of "haw-vuh" I have fought against the hokum that surrounds my profession.

To me, art is good art when it produces a worthy emotion, and if you are charmed by Rudy Vallee's rendition of *I'm Just a Vagabond Lover*, I shall not quarrel with you. The only persons I want exterminated are those who don't like any music of any kind.

All classical music is not good and all popular music is not bad, and the only way to judge singers and songs is to decide whether they do well the job they set out to perform.

THE GLORY ROAD

I like Rudy Vallee's singing. I think he is the best of the crooners. I admire Al Jolson. The expert harmony of the Duncan Sisters, singing *Remembering* in *Topsy and Eva*, moved me tremendously, and certainly was a more important contribution to art than the efforts of a mediocre pair of opera singers whom I heard a few nights later doing their best with the love duet in *Tristan und Isolde*.

There are singers of classical songs who have no little prestige but who leave their audiences utterly cold. Some of the patrons of the Metropolitan Opera Company would consider it sacrilege to mention Jolson and Vallee in the same breath with these inadequate operatic performers, but to me Jolson singing *Sonny Boy* is more truly a real artist than these near-greats ever have been or ever will be.

At the peak of all music I place the best operatic artists and the best classical music. But in my home, mixed with my most highly prized phonograph recordings of operatic masterpieces sung by Caruso and Amato, I have Paul Whiteman's orchestra, playing *When Day is Done* and *The Rhapsody in Blue*; Duke Ellington's *The Indigo Blues*, and Don Azpiazu's stirring reproduction of *The Peanut Vendor*.

When I was making *The Rogue Song* in Hollywood, every chance I got I dragged Clif Edwards (Ukulele Ike) into my dressing-room and made him play *St. Louis Blues*. Edwards has an amazing natural sense of rhythm, almost equaling that possessed by Bill Robinson, the syncopating Negro tap dancer, whose instinctive sense of rhythm is not surpassed even by that of Toscanini, the great operatic conductor.

I like all kinds of good music and I sing all kinds. I do not try to force any particular brand upon the public. If you get more pleasurable emotion when I sing Oley Speaks' *Sylvia* than when I sing Lully's somber aria, *Bois Enais*, I feel that it is no reflection on your intelligence. In fact, in many cases it is a real sign of superior mentality, because a lot of people who say they like *Bois Enais* are not intelligent at all—they're just *poseurs* and liars.

Frequently I sing *The Song of the Flea*, and every now and then, after a concert, well-meaning old ladies protest that it is quite vulgar. When I point out that the words are by Goethe and the music by Moussorgsky, they say, "Oh, that's different," and, all flustered, apologize. There's intellectual snobbery for you!

In my concerts I always sing one or two operatic numbers, because in the smaller cities the people do not get opera and they have a genuine love for the best operatic music. I do not, however, sing operatic numbers that are strange to the ears of the audience. In spite of the protests from some of my colleagues who say I am lowering myself, I sing usually either the prologue from *Pagliacci* or the toreador's song from *Carmen*, because—although I must admit I am a bit tired of them, myself—those are the two operatic numbers that are best liked by the great majority of non-professional music lovers.

I sing a few songs in French and German and Italian, because, in addition to the handful who really enjoy them, there are always a number of people in an audience who feel they have been classically cheated unless they have been given something they do not understand. They are the folks who believe that sulphur and molasses must be very good for you because it tastes so bad. So, when they hear music that gives them no sensation of pleasure whatsoever, they think it must be something of unusual merit and that, unless they applaud loudly, people will class them as ignoramuses. I like people who, when certain selections give them a pain in the neck, have the frankness to say so.

It is tradition around the Metropolitan Opera House that Caruso said people applauded his name and not his voice, and he proved it. In *Pagliacci* the Harlequin's serenade is sung off-stage by Beppe, a minor character. It brings no more than perfunctory applause. Unbeknown to the audience at the Metropolitan, at many a performance Caruso, as a joke, sang that off-stage aria, and not even the critics ever noticed that the serenade was sung in anything more than an adequate manner.

In Hollywood, at a party one evening at Charley Farrell's, we were sitting in the back yard (*patio* in Hollywood) and I was asked to sing. I stood up and improvised for five minutes, singing in an imitation of Russian—of which language I know not even one word. I sobbed, I laughed, I waved my arms, making up music and words as I went along. Finally I stopped, exhausted by my emotions.

They cheered and applauded like mad—Farrell, Virginia Valli, Paul Bern, Janet Gaynor, Robert Montgomery, Mr. and Mrs. Leslie Howard, and a dozen others.

"What is that?" they asked. "It's magnificent!"

"An operatic number by the Russian composer, Kovlikoffoskow-sky," I said, inventing a name.

"Beautiful!" they said.

It was not good music, because I am not a composer. And the words, of course, meant nothing.

An exotic movie actress, reputed to have been a member of the Russian nobility, grasped both my hands.

"Eet ees tremen-*dous!*" she cried. "My fav-rit aria!"

I nodded. "My Russian pronunciation isn't very good, though," I said.

"You are too mo-*dest*," she insisted. "I understood av-ry word!"

I let it go at that.

Perhaps the most popular tune ever written is Carrie Jacobs Bond's *A Perfect Day*. The fact that you may be sick and tired of it makes it no less a great song. I think the words are maudlin, but the music has real merit. Had it been trash, it would not have lived.

I had a long argument about it with Paul Gallico, a concert pianist and father of Paul Gallico, a New York sports writer. He had told me that my artistic standards were low because I sang Ethelbert Nevin's *Oh, That We Two Were Maying*. I knew it was a good song because it always made me weep—which is all I need to know about a song. When I told him what I thought about *A Perfect Day* he had a fit.

A year later I heard him play a Schumann sonata. This sonata begins with a strain that is definitely like the first phrases of *A Perfect Day*. If one was the work of genius, so was the other.

I pointed out to Gallico the parallel and sang the two tunes to him. "The trouble with you," I said, "is that you've read books in an effort to learn what you ought to like, instead of letting your own emotions and common sense do the judging."

He stuttered, scratched his head, and walked away.

As far as I can remember that's the only argument I ever won from a classical musician about *A Perfect Day*. But I'm still trying.

There is no reason why we should be apologetic about our American music.

Take *The Glory Road*, a Negro spiritual written by Jacques Wolfe, a music teacher in the public schools of Brooklyn, N. Y., who is no more a Southerner than was General Grant. I believe *The Glory Road* is just as fine a musical composition as Leoncavallo's prelude to *Pagliacci*. We have a number of popular patter songs that are as good as *La Donna è Mobile* from *Rigoletto*—Vincent Youmans' *Hallelujah*, for example.

We are leading the world in popular compositions. Jerome Kern's *Ol' Man River*, Youmans' *Without a Song*, and George Gershwin's *Rhapsody in Blue* equal anything ever written by the Viennese composers of operettas past and present, and surpass in real emotional musical quality half of the arias of standard operatic composers whose works are the backbone of every Metropolitan season.

Of course, we are producing a lot of rot. Tunes are being stolen and imitated. Generally our lyrics are gosh-awful. But the amount of good stuff is astounding.

The history of great music in all nations is that good popular music preceded good classical music. We are building a sound foundation, and one of these days Americans will be turning out operas that will live just as long as *Carmen* or *Tosca* or *Faust* or *Tristan und Isolde*.

We probably would be doing it now, were it not for the fact that composers and librettists have to eat, and the only real financial encouragement they receive comes from musical comedy and from the movies. The system of payment for the work of American operatic composers is murderous to genius. For instance, I doubt that Edna St. Vincent Millay and Deems Taylor in a lifetime will make as much money out of their splendid opera, *The King's Henchman*, as the authors of *Yes, We Have No Bananas* made during the first month the song was on sale.

Victor Herbert wrote *Natoma*, a fairly good grand opera, and could have turned out, I am sure, an operatic score of high rank and lasting quality if he had been willing for a year or two to give up the theater—which he loved and which made him rich and famous—and slave for the opera, which looked upon his genius with neither sympathy nor understanding.

If the millions of persons in America who are interested in better music could only be square with themselves they would encourage honest thinking and expression throughout the world of music. Impresarios, conductors, singers, musicians, composers, and librettists generally cannot express themselves naturally because, the moment they do, influential patrons inhibited by their confounded hokum complexes, unable to relax and to be on the level, will shake their heads and say, "Well, yes. I think I like it. But is it art?"

What nonsense!

The greatest music is that which thrills you most, and no one was ever really thrilled by sham and bombast and pretense.

I have heard magnificent symphony orchestras that left me weak in my chair, famous singers who raised my blood pressure almost to the point of apoplexy, mighty choruses that intoxicated me more than my first bottle of champagne, but I have never been so shaken emotionally as I was a few months ago by 1,500 Negro children singing in a high school auditorium in Birmingham, Ala.

They sang *Standin' in the Need of Prayer* and other spirituals, under the direction of an untrained Negro who knew none of the tricks, none of the "methods," who just believed that the way to sing was to throw yourself naturally into it and sing!

I was wrecked for the remainder of the day, and that night I gave one of the best concerts of my career because, from beginning to end, through classical selections and popular ones, I was inspired by the freedom and simplicity of those children.

They sang parts perfectly, with harmony as sure as that of a great pipe organ. I never heard such precision of attack, never such sheer vitality of tone. You could understand every word uttered by those 1,500 voices. Often at the Metropolitan Opera House, with only four persons singing at the same time, you can't catch a single phrase.

Those children sang for the joy of singing—just opened their throats and let go.

I was tingling all over. Shots of electricity went up and down my spine. My voice choked so that I couldn't speak. Tears ran down my cheeks.

Seldom at the Metropolitan, or at Carnegie Hall, have I found musical perfection, but certainly I found it in the auditorium of a Negro high school in Birmingham, where girls and boys sang superbly because they sang honestly.

If one of the patrons of the Metropolitan Opera had been standing there beside me and at the end had said, "Well, yes. I think I like it. But is it art?" I swear by all the gods that be, I would have killed him.

II

THEN ALONG CAME TWINS

I GOT my first important job as a singer, not particularly on account of my voice, but because I looked more like Charles Ray, the movie star, than did any of the eight other applicants.

It was at Grauman's Million Dollar movie theater in Los Angeles, which had just opened, and the show for the second week was a Charles Ray picture, the name of which I have forgotten. It was something about a blacksmith. Sid Grauman reproduced in a prologue a scene from the picture, and I was made up as a blacksmith and, accompanied by clanging anvils, sang a song in which I announced that shoeing horses was a very enviable life indeed.

I did so well that Grauman kept me for fifteen weeks, at $50 a week. The spick-and-span theater was equipped with all the latest gimcracks, including a huge orchestra platform that emerged from the pit on an elevator—the first one in the world, Sid said.

After the theater had been open two weeks, Grauman conceived a revolutionary idea in stagecraft. I rose out of the cellar with the orchestra, with the spotlight on me, singing *At Dawning*. I was supposed to be the sun, I believe, and in the darkened theater the house lights in rainbow colors crept up until they blazed forth in an effect that Sid said was just like the aurora borealis, only better. Larks sang and roosters crowed, and it certainly was something swell.

Sid said history was being made and that I should be very proud because I was the first singer in the world to be lifted out of an orchestra pit on an elevator. I *was* proud, too, although I still don't understand why he thought I looked like the sun. I wore a dress suit that had been given me by a high-school friend. It had belonged to his father, who had bought a new one after he discovered that the tailor had made a little mistake and had sold him a coat and trousers of two different kinds of broadcloth. No one ever seemed to notice the difference in material and I got by with that dress suit for years—until after my first year at the Metropolitan.

I lost my job when Grauman booked *The Golem*, a picture with Jewish atmosphere, and I failed utterly in my attempt to sing *Eili, Eili*, the Jewish lament. I never had heard it sung and delivered it rather coldly, not knowing much what the Hebrew words were about. Sid said I was terrible and hired a Jewish song plugger who put a moan into it and, he told me later, laid the audience sobbing in the aisles.

I was a struggling young husband, and that $50 a week had helped the Tibbett family get along rather well, although the birth of twins and resultant doctor's bills cut deep into the family fortune. The expenses would have been greater had it not been for the inspirational logic of my wife.

She had a woman doctor who had agreed on a price for the delivery. When twins came, the doctor sent a bill for double the amount, but my wife insisted that it was all one job and should be performed for one price, and I never did pay the added assessment.

Our first home was a cottage on the side of a hill in a vineyard at La Crescenta, fifteen miles from Los Angeles. The rent was $12.50 a month, and the landlord allowed us to eat all the grapes we wanted. There were times when we lived on grapes, and, strangely enough, I still like them. Our landlord also let me gather firewood from his property—you may have heard from the Los Angeles Chamber of Commerce that the nights are always cold—and once when I was $75 behind in my rent he let me pay out by working in the vineyard.

We thought our home was a mansion, but perhaps we were not good judges of mansions. I rented a piano for $5 a month, and when the men brought it I told them to put it in the living-room, which was on stilts, extending out over the side of the hill. They took one look at the stilts and said they wouldn't risk their piano on such insecure footing. They were afraid it would fall through the floor and roll down the hill. So we put it in the bedroom, which rested on solid ground.

Since I never had known anything about luxury, I was well content to struggle along in what, as I look back, seems to have been at times very close to real poverty.

The earliest days of my life were spent in Bakersfield, Calif., which then was a tiny, raw, tough town in the center of a farming community. Later, with the arrival of the oil boom, it was destined to become a prosperous city, but unfortunately the Tibbett family had no share in that prosperity, for, by the time Bakersfield's oil was flowing freely, we had moved away.

Had we remained we might have become rich, like many of our neighbors, and it would not have been necessary for me, later, to borrow nearly $8,000, which, added to the money I was able to earn with my voice, plus contributions of generous patrons, was the cost of turning me into a self-supporting singer.

We lived in a frame cottage at 716 K Street, on the edge of Bakersfield—my parents, my two brothers, my sister, and myself. I was the youngest.

My parents and my uncles and aunts—with the exception of Uncle Ed—were strict Methodists. I was taught to believe that dancing, smoking, drinking, card playing, and the theater were instruments of the devil. I don't remember how the family justified Uncle Ed, who kept Bakersfield's leading saloon. As far as I can remember nobody looked upon him with disapproval. He was a gay, witty fellow and always welcome to the family councils.

I am sure that, had my father lived, he would have opposed my ambition to get into the theater. Some time after he died my mother confessed apprehensively that she really thought the theater was a delightful place to go. My mother wanted me to become a physician, but when she found I was interested only in the stage, with the enthusiastic co-operation of my sister, Betty Lee, she helped me have my own way.

My mother sang in the Methodist church choir in Bakersfield and it was she who first taught me to sing. We were all interested in music. My sister played the piano, my brother Jesse played the mandolin, and my brother Ernest sang very well.

My father was a God-fearing man with a large blond mustache, who believed in strict law and order. It was a family of law enforcers. Even Uncle Ed now and then stepped from behind his bar and joined a posse in pursuit of an outlaw. My Uncle George at one time was sheriff of Kern County, in which Bakersfield is situated, and Uncle Bert—now a detective in Bakersfield—was a deputy sheriff. My father, in his early life a farmer, was later deputy sheriff, then sheriff, and for several years a range rider for the Kern County Land Company, guarding fences and chasing rustlers. He was a dead shot, a splendid horseman, and had killed two cattle thieves.

We had horses and chickens and cows, a setter dog named "Mart" and a bloodhound named "Rod." The bloodhound was a highly bred man-hunter which lived in canine luxury and was ready at any moment to start on the trail of a fugitive. We kids were never allowed to play with him for fear it might soften his reputedly brutal nature. Whenever my father took him out, Rod would sniff the scent, dig all four feet into the ground, tug eagerly at the leash, and bay furiously, with eyes afire.

My father, dragged behind, would wave an arm and shout ominously, "Rod's got him this time!"

But invariably Rod would lead the heavily armed posse to the feet of some innocent-eyed cow or to a coyote den under a pile of brush. That bloodhound promised more and delivered less than any animal I ever saw. He would have made an ideal bond salesman, I'm sure.

Of course my father was my hero, and when we kids played "sheriff and rustlers" in the back yard, I was always the sheriff. I gained the honor without contest for the other boys wanted to be Jim McKinney, an outlaw whose name was a more dreadful phrase in Bakersfield than Billy the Kid's in New Mexico and Arizona. Jim McKinney had killed four men in cold blood.

One day, when I was seven years old, our gang was playing in the back yard, camping out—roasting potatoes and getting ready for a battle.

I saw a man drive up in a buggy. He entered the house, and a moment later hurried out with my mother and they drove rapidly toward town. I gave it little thought for I had important work to do—there were "rustlers" hiding back of the barn and "Sheriff" Lawrence Tibbett had to shine up his wooden gun.

Suddenly an older boy came running up the dusty road, leaped the fence, and yelled at me, "Hey, Larry, Jim McKinney just killed your father!"

At first I thought it was a joke, part of a game.

"Honest!" the boy insisted, all out of breath. "Cross my heart and hope to die! In the Chinese joss house! Your father went after Jim, and Jim got him! They carried him to Baer's drug store! I seen him!"

The emotions of boys are unfathomable. I cannot explain the apparent lack of grief with which I met the announcement. I never have been able to understand why I was not at once crushed. But I did not feel at all like crying. I was only very, very proud. Perhaps a psychoanalyst can explain my pride. I cannot. It was not until that evening that I realized my loss.

McKinney had been ordered out of Bakersfield a few days before, and my father had enforced the order. He got the drop on McKinney, and the bandit, humiliated, galloped away with bullets from my father's six-shooter kicking up the dust behind him.

To show his contempt, McKinney promptly robbed a stage near Bakersfield, and my father headed a posse sent out to get him. They chased him through the mountains and found that McKinney had circled back to Bakersfield to see his sweetheart.

Father led the posse into the Chinese joss house where McKinney was hiding. Father was too brave and too reluctant to kill. Instead of shooting on sight, he ordered McKinney to come out. McKinney killed my father with a shotgun and killed Jeff Packard, the sheriff, who came to my father's rescue. But my Uncle Bert got Jim McKinney, with a shot right between the eyes.

A few years ago I was cast to sing Jack Rance, the sheriff, in a revival of *The Girl of the Golden West* at the Metropolitan Opera House in New York. This was the part sung by Amato when the opera was first produced in 1910. Caruso and Emmy Destinn were in the original cast.

In the revival Martinelli sang the tenor rôle and Jeritza sang Minnie.

Puccini's opera is beautifully done, but, after all, it is an Italian's conception of the Wild West, and the music is by no means Western in manner or feeling. A German director was staging the revival at the Metropolitan and the cowboys didn't act like any cowboys I had ever seen—either around Bakersfield or on my uncle's ranch in the Tejon Mountains, where, as a youngster, I had done some cow-punching myself. For instance, in the celebration at the end of the opera the director had these supposedly tough cow hands throw their arms around one another and express their jubilation by kissing each other on the cheek in the best Latin manner.

In the scene where the sheriff enters the cabin, searching for Johnson, the bandit, the director told me to come in crouching, with my six-shooter held at arm's length in front of me. I obeyed, and felt more like Annette Kellerman doing the Australian crawl than I did like a sheriff.

"This will never do," I said. "The sheriff would enter standing erect, on the alert, with the gun held at his hip so he can swing it quickly to any part of the room."

"Poof!" the director said. "What does an opera singer know about sheriffs?"

I told him what I knew about sheriffs.

"Oh," he said apologetically, and shrank away from me. "Oh. Then we shall do it your way."

Upon my advice he eliminated the cowboy osculation in the last act, too, and forever after seemed to be a bit afraid of me. I believe he did not entirely understand my English. He thought I was the one who had done all the killing I had told him about, and he guessed he had better be good to me or I'd run amuck and shoot up the Metropolitan Opera House.

My father had $10,000 in life insurance, and my mother took us to Long Beach, Calif., where she tried to support the family by running a small hotel. Five years later she sold the hotel at a loss and we moved to Los Angeles. Curiously enough, like Bakersfield, Long Beach became a great oil town—after, alas, my mother had sold her property.

I was twelve years old when we left Long Beach. Kindly but inaccurate biographers have said that I helped to support the family by working as a bell boy in my mother's hotel and by selling papers. I did both, but we were not so poor that my efforts were any help. The most I ever made in one day by selling papers was 15 cents, and I was so proud of myself that I went immediately to a drug store and spent it all on a banana split.

While we were at Long Beach I was caught smoking corn silk, and my deeply religious aunts and uncles, who were visiting us, raised as much fuss as though I had kidnapped Marlene Dietrich's baby. I was so frightened that, with very few exceptions, I have never smoked from that day to this. As I grew older my mother would reinforce my principles by telling me that if I smoked I would never be a good singer; but a great many singers smoke, and their voices do not seem to suffer. Caruso and Scotti smoked constantly. Martinelli never smokes, nor do any of the women who sing at the Metropolitan.

About once a year I smoke one cigar, and get great satisfaction out of the feeling that I am doing something terribly wrong and that the devil is patting me on the back. Now and then I have sung parts in which the character has to smoke.

Jeritza and Rosa Ponselle are almost the only singers at the Metropolitan who are terribly afraid that smoke will harm their voices. In *The Girl of the Golden West* the sheriff is supposed to smoke a big cigar. Before the first performance Jeritza asked me not to smoke while she was on the stage, but I did not realize that she meant that I wasn't to smoke at all. Previous to her first entrance I had taken a few dramatic and satisfying puffs. The smoke had vanished, but she smelled it. She sniffed, glared at me, and then began coughing violently, missing her music cue, so that the orchestra had to stop. After that, I just chewed my cigar. I know when to take a hint.

My mother bought a big house at Twelfth and Figueroa Streets in Los Angeles and took in roomers. Whenever she had time to spare she went out as a practical nurse. My brothers married when they were quite young, and Betty Lee and I were the only children at home. Betty Lee taught me how to play the piano a little, taught me songs, and when, at thirteen, I began taking piano lessons from a professional teacher she joined her threats of violence with my mother's and forced me to practice.

I learned to sing, among other things, *I Love You Truly, Just a-Wearyin' for You*, and *Sing Me to Sleep*, and at the age of fourteen I was able to stand up in the parlor and knock callers cold with my own conception of *The Rosary*.

Although I loved to sing, in my high-school days at Manual Arts in Los Angeles, my ambition was to become an actor. The movies were just beginning to get a toe hold in Hollywood, but at that time I scorned what seemed to be a trivial and transitory toy and I was not interested in lending the support of a Tibbett to those one-reel dramas that were being shown in nickelodeons. It was late in my high-school days when D. W.

Griffith gave in Los Angeles the world première of *The Clansman*—later known as *The Birth of a Nation*—which sent all of us kids flocking to the studios in a futile effort to get in on the ground floor in this newly discovered art.

I was taught to take great pride in the family name. My ancestors had come to California in the gold rush of '49 and the name had never been sullied.

All my relatives spell it "Tibbet"—with one "t." A careless or disinterested proofreader turned it into "Tibbett." That was the way it appeared on the program of the Metropolitan Opera House the night I first sang a real part—Valentine in *Faust*.

Frank La Forge, my teacher, noticed the mistake in spelling, after the performance, and said, "It looks better that way. You should keep that spelling."

I let it stand, and ever since have been "Tibbett" instead of "Tibbet."

My family protested furiously. It was sacrilege! Wasn't the name that was good enough for my forefathers good enough for me?

I shudder when I think what they would have said had I followed the advice of some of my friends, who told me in all seriousness that I could never get anywhere at the Metropolitan with an American name, and that I should change it to Lorenzo Tibbetto. Frank La Forge and Rupert Hughes, who were my ever-present friends in trouble, both reinforced my belief that if I was to succeed it should be as an American and that I should not be swayed by people who were servile to the flapdoodle of so-called European prestige.

Since I successfully snubbed that suggestion, I think I should be allowed to feed my vanity when it hungers for just one extra "t."

In 1920 in Los Angeles, I played Iago in a local production of *Othello*, and had myself listed on the program as Lawrence Mervil. Since Mervil is my middle name, my mother and sister didn't protest very much. They just thought it was silly.

I believed that "Lawrence Mervil" was something very hot—a really distinguished name for an actor. The critics praised Lawrence Mervil, and I went around with clippings in my hands pointing out that Lawrence Mervil in reality was none other than myself. People read the clippings, looked at my long neck and my thin body and my childlike face, and said "You? Iago?" and didn't believe me. So I went back to my real name.

Since I have been at the Metropolitan, I have crusaded militantly against the warped fanatics who worship all that is European in opera and who are ashamed of all that is American. I have been fortunate in that I have been able to give whatever talent I may possess in furthering the success of such fine American operas as *The King's Henchman*, *Peter Ibbetson*, and *The Emperor Jones*.

On the other hand I have been a party to the criminal acts of performing *in German* a story of an American Negro jazz singer, *Jonny Spielt Auf*, and, *in Italian, The Girl of the Golden West!* In the latter opera I always took secret pleasure in the fact that there were two American words that could not be translated into Italian—"whisky" and "Wells Fargo"—and when I came to one of those words I would roar it out, maliciously, double forte, till the rafters of the Metropolitan rang and the diamond necklaces in the boxes shook with terror as though—I hoped—their owners had heard the bugle call of the revolution.

I was the first American male singer to rise to leading rôles at the Metropolitan without European training, and I hope I have blazed a trail that soon will become a broad highway.

Many American singers are cursed with this feeling of shame when they sing in English. I can roar out "I *love* you!" with all the passion of a Don Juan whose lady love is confined on a desert at the top of a high tower. But many American singers cannot become emotional in English. They will put their very souls into *Io t'amo, Ich liebe dich*, and *Je t'aime,* but on "I love you" they stammer like a schoolboy with his first sweetheart.

Members of our best Puritan families, with librettos in their hands, so that they cannot in any way pretend they do not understand the ribald goings on, will applaud scenes and lines, done in a foreign language, that if performed in English would bring the patrol wagon clanging to the stage door. I maintain that if an opera is vulgar in English it is vulgar in Italian, but even in Los Angeles, one of the strongholds of Puritanism, I have performed *The Jest,* which contains more sizzling lines and scenes than the ones that sent Mae West to jail. And the Best People and their débutante daughters applauded the Italian text with complete approval.

In high school I first began to realize that other boys wore better clothes than I, that they had money to spend, and that they were sought after by girls—while nobody seemed to pay any attention to me. I then appreciated, too, the sacrifices that my mother was making for me, and I tried to help out by working Saturdays and Sundays in the office of a Los Angeles newspaper, stuffing comics and magazine sections into Sunday newspapers, and counting classified ads.

I developed an inferiority complex, which at that time was a very good thing for me, because I worked furiously as a member of the glee and dramatic clubs in an effort to show the other students that I amounted to something, even though I had only one suit of clothes and couldn't afford to treat the crowd at the corner drug store.

Maude Howell, a beautiful girl, just out of Leland Stanford, came to Manual Arts as a dramatic teacher. All the kids, including myself, instantly fell in love with her, and the dramatic classes were filled to overflowing. She had real talent, and later went to New York, where she played a number of important parts in Broadway shows and then became a stage director—the first woman stage director that New York ever saw. She worked with George Arliss, and when he went into the movies he took her to Hollywood with him. She is still one of the most important members of his staff. When I made *The Prodigal* and *New Moon* in Hollywood, I borrowed her from Mr. Arliss, and she coached my acting and my dialogue.

Miss Howell gave me my first lessons in acting, taught me the importance of exact characterization, and instilled in me an ambition to do a real job on the stage. Had I not had this early training I am sure that my efforts in grand opera would have been less successful, for I have always tried to be an actor as well as a singer.

In high school I sang in the glee club and acted in a score of plays. I played Romeo and Marc Antony and was in Synge's *Riders to the Sea*, and never did learn how to pronounce the author's name.

In the glee club, Glen Meneley, now in lyceum work, was our best singer. Helen Jerome Eddy was our best actress, and after graduating went into the movies at a salary that made your head swim—$100 a week! And Phyllis Haver stepped out of school into a Mack Sennett bathing suit.

I failed to make the glee club the first year. That was my first artistic setback, for, encouraged by my friends, I had expected to be welcomed as God's gift to the Manual Arts glee club. It taught me a lesson. Never since that day have I believed in the gushing praises of my friends. I wait for the morning papers!

At that time I did not have an unusual voice. In fact, I did not develop the spark until after I was twenty-one years old—which may be a note of encouragement, or perhaps of despair, to those fathers and mothers whose children are now going about the house yodeling ambitiously.

As I look back now I often wonder why and how I ever kept at it. I was always struggling to get a part in a play or a place in a high-school concert. There was always somebody who undoubtedly was better than I. No matter how hard I tried in high school I never reached the top.

It must have been my inborn love for singing that carried me on. Certainly, not until years later did it ever occur to me that I might some day sing at the Metropolitan Opera House. Even now I am somewhat dazed by my success, and sometimes I feel that all this surely must be only temporary and that the next time I sing a high A flat my voice will shatter into a thousand pieces.

When I sit down to look in a detached manner at myself I know that it all came about merely because, with the help of others, I did what I wanted to do. And perhaps that's the secret of success.

I was in bad health when I entered high school and my mother was afraid I was tubercular. I did not have the vocal strength necessary for good singing. I put a horizontal bar in the back yard and learned to perform big drops and little drops and to hang by my heels. I tried out for athletic teams, put the shot, wrestled, played rugby, and swam until I had the lungs of a fish peddler.

Since then I have always been in good physical condition. You can't sing powerfully throughout a performance unless you have a diaphragm like a heavyweight wrestler's. On tour I always carry a folding rowing machine with me, and every morning in my room I row—it seems to me —from New York to Albany.

One of the boys I admired most in high school was Jimmy Doolittle, who turned out to be probably the world's greatest aviator. I was a rather frail, timid boy and Jimmy was the embodiment of all I wished to be. He had a thorough contempt for most would-be actors and singers but still we were good friends. He was a good boxer—later amateur champion middleweight of southern California—a member of the wrestling and tumbling teams and a dashing, smashing youngster who was not afraid of man, woman, devil, or professor.

Even then Jimmy was interested in aviation. We would argue militantly about whether flying was more important than singing, and I always lost the argument. Rob Wagner, the artist, writer, and moving picture director, taught art and wrestling at high school. I entered his wrestling class, in which Jimmy was the star pupil, and one afternoon tried out for the wrestling team.

Jimmy was standing at one side of the gymnasium.

"Hello, crow," I said.

"Hi, nightingale," he sniffed.

"See what Larry can do, Jimmy," said Wagner.

There was a swish, and I was flat on my back on the mat and Jimmy was walking away brushing his palms. He turned and looked at my sprawling body.

"For gosh sake, sing," he said.

The next day I transferred from Wagner's wrestling class to his art class.

I met Jimmy at a Lambs' Gambol in New York a few years ago. He shook my hand and said, "I went to a concert of yours a few weeks ago just to find out."

"To find out what?"

"If that Tibbett kid that used to squawk around Manual Arts was really the same Tibbett I'd read in the papers about. I couldn't believe it. Honest, Larry, you're not nearly as bad as I thought you'd be."

Last year I found myself in trouble in Dallas. Trains were delayed by floods and I had to be in St. Louis for a concert the next evening. Jimmy happened to be in the vicinity and I called him up and asked for help. He responded instantly and, it seemed to me, had me in St. Louis in about twenty minutes.

Soon after we left the ground he yelled back at me, "Y'know, I'm glad of this chance. This is a new plane and I wanted to try it out. It's never been flown before, and a lot of people said if I tried to get 175 miles an hour out of it, the ship would fall apart." He pointed to the speed indicator. We were going 205.

Leaving school, I picked up various odd jobs, acting and singing. I was beginning to find my voice. I did very well in church choirs and at funerals. I got $35 a week, for two weeks out of the month, as a member of the cast of the Civic Repertoire Company. We had guest stars from the movies—Milton Sills, Henry Walthall, Helen Jerome Eddy, and

Lionel Belmore—and I stood in awe of these masters and studied their technique as a golfer studies Bobby Jones' swing. I usually played old men with whiskers because I wasn't handsome enough to play young heroes.

I had a small part in a company headed by Mr. and Mrs. Tyrone Power, who were giving a program of selected scenes from Shakespeare. After a successful week in Los Angeles, the show was to go on a long tour, but folded after one night in Pasadena. I think dear old superstitious Mr. and Mrs. Power blamed me, for in Pasadena I violated two of the most important rules laid down by actors: I whistled in my dressing-room and then went on the stage before the performance and looked through the peek-hole in the curtain and counted the house—which didn't take long.

I still whistle in my dressing-room and cannot trace any further misfortune to this idiosyncrasy, although it shocks my Italian dresser, who, in spite of all I can do, tries to ward off the hoodoo by forcing me to put on my right shoe before my left one. It seems that when bad luck is hovering around, it flees when it sees a man with his right shoe on and his left shoe off.

When the United States entered the war I joined the navy to see the world, and for nearly a year saw almost nothing but San Francisco Bay from the deck of the training ship, Iris. After four months I had been made an "instructor in seamanship," which was a very fine title for a most unimportant job. I taught the rookies how to row a boat, scrub decks, paint the ship, and tie knots. I also led a ship's quartet in the singing of rowdy songs, regarding which I was more proficient than at the art of holystoning a deck.

Eventually I managed to get a transfer to the Boylston, and was in Baltimore when the war ended. I returned to San Francisco by rail and, instead of being discharged, was sent to Vladivostok on a leaky ship named the Caderetta, heavily laden with ammunition and supplies for American soldiers and a locomotive for Kerensky.

Six months after she left San Francisco, the Caderetta was back again. It was May 15, 1919. I was twenty-two years old, weary and homesick. I was discharged at once, and four days later, in Los Angeles, married Grace Mackay Smith, who had boarded several years with my mother and whom I had first known in high school.

It was a marriage of impulse and we were fortunate, indeed, that it lasted as long as it did. In 1931, after we had discussed divorce for several years, Grace and I finally admitted that it was no go and that we would be happier apart.

The wedding plans were conceived at a party celebrating my homecoming, and Grace and I were married the following day. One of the guests at the party, Arthur Millier, now art critic of the *Los Angeles Times*, was best man. We had planned a double wedding, but he and his bride-to-be changed their minds. They were married soon after—but not to each other.

I had saved $500. Grace's grandmother, who for several years before and after our marriage sent her fifty dollars a month, gave us a small car as a wedding present. I bought a new suit for $15, and we two crazy kids drove to Portland, Ore., on our honeymoon, and when we returned all that was left of the $500 was $2.35 and a memory of what seemed to us to have been as lavish a honeymoon as any millionaire newlyweds ever had!

My mother, not expecting me from Vladivostok so soon had gone to Dallas to visit relatives and I did not see her until we returned from our honeymoon. She was too poor to give us anything like a motorcar, but her wedding present was some linen for us both, a watch for me—the first one I ever had—and to Grace my mother gave her choicest possession—an enlarged portrait in a gilded frame showing me in a little lace dress at the age of two years.

Although our marriage did not last forever it was an adventure and an important event in my life. When I was married I was a dreamer and wanted to sit under a palm tree and philosophize. If I had had no responsibilities I probably would still be sitting under that same palm tree, waiting for the fruit to drop, instead of taking off my shoes and climbing up after it.

Grace had courage, dash, ambition. She was temperamental—much more so than I. She had an unerring sense of comedy, real acting ability. She was witty and would have made a great *comédienne* had she been given the opportunity. Her real ambition, however, was to write, and no less an authority than Rupert Hughes said she had marked ability as a poetess.

We had some very, very good times together—and some awfully rotten ones. We were both mercurial in our dispositions. I had my singing; she had her poetry. When we were both succeeding, all was well, but when I came home at night after a performance with which I was not satisfied, and she had spent the evening searching unsuccessfully for poetic inspiration, we would greet each other sourly, and, like "Mr. and Mrs." in the cartoon, we would argue long into the night about nothing that really mattered at all.

When I was married I was a callow youngster with an idea that a husband should be the head of a family, and without any knowledge as to the way to acquire that position diplomatically. Grace had vitality and force, and at once took charge of me. Manlike, I thought I was henpecked and did my best to dominate, to be the big IT of the family. I thought my singing was something of international importance and that everything else should be subordinated to that. She made me battle for the position of head of the family, and these battles, I think, very often gave me backbone and confidence to step out into the world and keep my head up as I fought for my own career.

I wanted her to praise my singing, and she did. At times she seemed to be the only person in the world who thought I was any good. But, in turn, I did not praise her poetry. I was so selfishly immersed in my own work that I thought I had no time to encourage her art.

I was thoroughly inconsistent. In the first years of our married life

I cheerfully—well, perhaps not cheerfully, but at least without complaining *much!*—stood over a steaming tub and washed the twins' diapers, but I refused to get up in the middle of the night when the babies cried.

When we were married, Grace was employed as a stenographer and continued to work for about four months after our wedding. When our twins were born, one weighed 4¾ pounds and the other 4¼ pounds. Today they are fine, strong, healthy boys and the pride of my life.

Both have fine voices and, I hope, will develop real ambitions for artistic careers. I shall be very, very proud if they take a serious interest in making music and the stage their life work.

When I first left Los Angeles to study in New York, I did not have enough money to take the family along, and Grace went to work again in Los Angeles, but after two months found it was better for all concerned if she stayed at home and cared for the twins. My efforts to conquer New York were being financed by loans from a generous patron and, to the small amount of money that I was able to send back from New York, he added enough to keep my wife and children through the critical period, until I made sufficient to support my family and to help my mother a little. It was not until I got into the movies, however—years later—that I was able to pay back the money I had borrowed.

When it became evident that the complete happiness of both our lives could be restored only by separation, Grace and I took the sane, sensible road and she established a residence in Reno and our marriage was dissolved. We share my income and now, enjoying the luxuries that were denied us in our early days, she, as well as I, can pursue a career free from material worry or interruption. She recently published a book of poems and I hope sincerely that she is on the verge of real success.

Soon after we were married, I began to miss the sea. Not that I had any particular love for an ocean life, but I had found that I was enormously stimulated by standing at the prow of a pitching ship and singing into the storm. Singing teachers say you must never open your mouth in the wind, which, I think, is a superstition.

I would get on my bicycle and ride to the hills, climb a sandy peak, and roar into the night breezes.

Ten years later I reported for work at the Metro-Goldwyn-Mayer moving picture studio.

A publicity man, gathering data, asked me, "Where did you come from?"

"Right here," I said.

"You mean, you used to live in Los Angeles?"

"For years and years," I said.

He was a bit astonished.

"Well—er," he said, "where did you do the best singing of your career? At the Metropolitan?"

I took him by the arm and led him outside my dressing-room. I pointed to the huge group of buildings in front of us.

"I used to ride a bicycle right across this property," I said, "and—see that hill over there? That's where I sang better than at any other place in the world."

A few weeks later I made a sentimental journey in a motorcar over to that hill and sang into the wind, but it was a flat performance. It was utterly uninspired, and I got no satisfaction out of it whatsoever. The landscape was in no way as magnificent as I had remembered it, and the hill seemed to have shrunk.

Had I ridden over there on a bicycle and pumped my way to the top, instead of gliding up in a motorcar, the view from the heights probably would have seemed worth while. Perhaps there's some pretty sound philosophy about life in general, in that experience. If I had a palm tree under which to dream, I would develop it.

III

THEY PUT ME IN JAIL FOR SINGING

A T various times in my early career I was shy and awed at the prospect of appearing with such famous women as Jeritza, Alda, Ponselle, and Bori, but the only leading woman who really had me scared to death was Lupe Velez, in the movies.

After I signed my contract to make *The Cuban Love Song*, they told me at the studio that I was to work with a splendid cast, including Jimmy Durante and Ernest Torrence, which was very good news indeed.

I have never shared with some actors and singers the idea that the worse the supporting cast, the better for the star. An audience, I believe, goes to the theater to see a good show, with good actors in every part, and the star who thinks people like to pay money to see him attempt to put over an entire performance single-handed is riding for a fall. Even in concerts, the successful singer must have the assistance of the most talented pianist he can find.

I once heard an actor complaining that Marie Dressler had stolen his picture.

"I wish," I said, "I could get her to steal one of mine."

Torrence, whose recent death shocked me tremendously, was a real friend and a magnificent actor. Durante is a natural comedian, and in New York night clubs had given me many laughs. Up to that time he had made only one picture, which he stole from William Haines, the star, and I knew Jimmy was working violently to make good in the movies.

"Whom have you in mind for the leading woman?" I asked.

"Lupe Velez," they said.

"Lupe Velez!" I swallowed three times. "You mean the Mexican wildcat who hit a director over the head with a bottle!"

"None other. She will play the peanut vender, and she'll be so hot that she'll melt the steel in the proscenium arch and it'll come blopping down upon the orchestra!"

Up to that time, as leading woman, I had had Catherine Dale Owen in *The Rogue Song*, Grace Moore in *New Moon*, and Esther Ralston in *The Prodigal*, none of whom, as far as I knew, ever hit anybody over the head with a bottle.

"Listen," I said, "there has been a terrible mistake. My name is Lawrence Tibbett. I'm a singer. You evidently have me mixed up with Sam Houston, who licked the Mexican army!"

They said no, they knew who I was and they were going to bill me as the great lover of the Metro-Goldwyn-Mayer lot, and that in the picture Lupe and I had some flaming love scenes which would make the Chicago fire look like a burnt match.

"That," I said, "is out. I'm no great lover. I'm just an opera singer trying to get along in the movies."

We compromised. The great-lover publicity thereupon died unborn, but, if she chose, the dynamic Lupe was to go boiling through the story like Mt. Etna on a rampage.

I went around asking everybody, "What's the best way for me to get along with Lupe Velez?"

I might as well have asked, "What's the best way to jump over the moon?" It couldn't be done.

They warned me, "She's likely to bust out any minute, kick over the camera, and pick up a light and swat you over the head."

When we first met at rehearsal she seemed to appraise me with a challenging eye.

"How do you do?" I said, knowing very well how she did.

She said she did all right, which was contrary to what I had heard.

Then came an inspiration from heaven! I offered, "I understand that you have a lovely voice." I knew nothing about her voice.

"Who told you that?" she demanded.

Something in her tone indicated that, shooting blindly, I had struck a vital spot. I was to learn, thank God, that she did have a good voice.

"Everybody," I answered.

"It is not like my mother's," Lupe said quietly. "Her voice was divine. She was an opera singer in Mexico."—She looked up at me. "Would you sing something for Lupe some time? Something in Spanish, perhaps?"

"Of course," I said, with what little breath was left in my body. "How about now? There's a piano over there."

I felt as Clyde Beatty, the animal trainer, must have felt when he first made a tiger lie down and roll over. Now I believed Congreve— "Music hath charms to soothe the savage breast, to soften rocks, or bend a knotted oak."

I have never worked more peacefully with a leading woman. Flushed by music's success with Lupe, I made up my mind that I would go out and try it on a rock and a knotted oak, but I never got around to it.

Lupe Velez is a great emotional actress. Her only trouble is that she believes what the press agents write about her, and acts off-stage as well as on in a desperate and doubtless tiring effort to live up to her reputation as a firebrand.

Our only difficulty with her was in getting her to sing a song in the picture. Believe it or not, Lupe was too shy! Away from the microphone she sang beautifully. She knew good music, and could imitate an opera singer and sing cadenzas and top notes and hit a clear, free top C as well as many a coloratura. But when the sound apparatus was turning over, time and again, before she finally recorded her song perfectly, she broke down and ran off the set, crying, "Lupe is not engaged to be a singer! She cannot do it!"

Only recently she and Jimmy Durante made a great hit, in person, in the musical comedy, *Strike Me Pink*, and she proved there that she had a fine natural voice.

Durante was a genial, willing, likable roughneck, new to the movies and ready to break a leg for the camera if it would get him a laugh. He was so determined to deliver the goods that he ran around asking advice of everybody on the lot, and believed everything they told him. He was meat for the practical jokers.

One day W. S. Van Dyke, director of *The Cuban Love Song*, after setting the stage for the job and prompting a dozen people, from the chief costumer to Louis Mayer, the big boss, told Jimmy that the next day he was to play a Bulgarian general in a love scene with Lupe Velez.

Jimmy was highly pleased. "Romeo stuff, hey?" he said, spitting on his hands. "Watch Durante!"

Van Dyke told Jimmy to go to the wardrobe department to get his costume.

Jimmy came back staggering under a load. He wore a golden helmet, much too large for him, with eagles on it and a yellow plume four feet long. He had a mighty sword that dragged on the ground. His coat was bright red with yellow epaulettes, and his chest sank under a score of medals. Across his breast were six bright ribbons and around his waist a red, white, and blue sash. His trousers were pink and were almost hidden in patent-leather hip boots, to which were attached flopping spurs that interfered with Jimmy's feet, so that he had to take zigzag steps, like an Indian dodging bullets. Swinging from a gold cord around his neck was a tuba.

The make-up man had painted Jimmy's long nose a bright blue and had put black circles under his eyes and a goatee on his chin.

Jimmy was not in the scenes we were shooting that day, but never worked harder in his life.

"How is it?" he asked Van Dyke.

"Magnificent!" said Van Dyke.

"On de level?" said Jimmy. "I t'ot maybe it was a little loud."

"It's colossal. But you'd better go back and put on blue pants. They're more regal than pink."

The pants changed, he was sent to Louis Mayer. Mayer ordered the medals shifted from the left breast to the right, which, it seemed, was the proper spot for medals in Bulgaria. Irving Thalberg, another big boss called into consultation, sent him to the prop department for a longer sword.

Jimmy, sweating, anxious to please, eagerly obeyed every order, and for half a day ran from executive to costume department, to prop room, to executive.

"T'ink it's better now?" he would inquire hopefully, wiping the perspiration from his eyes, only to be met with further changes.

At last he caught someone snickering. He realized what was going on.

"Hey," he demanded, "what's dis, a gag?"

"It's a gag, Jimmy," somebody confessed.

He grinned sheepishly, then turned toward a mirror, threw back his shoulders, and slapped his chest. "Well," he said, "gag or no gag, I never saw Durante look sweller!"

Torrence, Durante, and I had a big scene in a shell hole in No Man's Land. I sang *From the Halls of Montezuma to the Shores of Tripoli*, the most stirring military song that we have. It should be our national anthem.

I was supposed to go crazy and try to run over and lick the entire German army. Bombs burst around us, almost burying us in dirt and cork stones. Torrence worked so hard that he fainted, and had to be revived by the emergency crew. A shell exploded in front of me while I was singing, and I finished the song with my mouth full of mud.

There were hundreds of extras, great batteries of lights, and the scene cost thousands of dollars.

We felt that we had done a good job, and the next day asked to see the "rushes," as they called the unedited shots.

"Oh, didn't you hear?" said the assistant director. "The cameramen balled things up, so it isn't any good."

"Do you mean that we have to do all that over again?" I asked.

"Oh, no," he said. "They can't afford it. They've decided to do without the scene."

Jimmy Durante was standing near. He shook a finger in the assistant director's face. "You can't fool Durante," he said. "You guys never was goin' to use the scene! Some day you practical jokers will go too far!"

To this day he may still believe it was a gag to make us do all that hard work for nothing.

It was about this time that I learned that while music may soften rocks and bend a knotted oak, it has no effect upon the heart of a police judge. Nor will it melt iron bars. I was jailed for singing!

Four of us started to sing, late one night, in a Los Angeles restaurant. The proprietor told us to shut up. One of my friends pointed out to the proprietor that I was to sing a few weeks later at the Auditorium, that seats were selling for $7.70 each, and that the restaurant-keeper should be proud to have my voice echoing through his halls. He said it was just a lot of noise to him, and we'd have to "scram" or he'd call the cops.

On the sidewalk my friend, the self-appointed director-general of the party, started a loud quarrel with a passing Negro, and in a moment we were surrounded by policemen, who had been called by someone in the restaurant.

The four of us were locked up in the Wilshire police station, where I said my name was Mervil Lawrence. I might have called friends to get me out, but the director-general said he was a man of great influence in Los Angeles and that he would fix everything—keep the story out of the newspapers and have us freed, with profuse apologies from the police.

He showed me a gold badge to prove his importance and I was impressed, though later I remembered that he had shown the badge to the police and they had immediately taken us to the station.

Since I was sure everything was to come out all right, I looked upon it as a gay adventure. In my cell I sang *The Prisoner's Song, Tenting on the Old Camp Ground*, the prison song from *Faust*—all three parts, soprano, tenor, and bass—and, at the request of a pickpocket, *Frankie and Johnny*.

The other prisoners applauded heartily. I have never had a more appreciative audience than those vagabonds who got a $7.70 concert for nothing.

We went to court in the patrol wagon in the morning. I began to have a few misgivings about the power of my friend who was going to fix everything, and I was quite startled when the judge, instead of apologizing, fined my friend $75 and the other three of us $25 each.

And in the director-general's efforts to reach influential editors to kill the story, he had only tipped them off, and I fled from the courthouse with a newspaper over my head to shield me from the cameras.

Strangely enough, I was still under the spell of my friend's promise to fix the newspapers, and I explained to my wife that I had been up with a sick friend, that my car had broken down, and that I had been rehearsing all night, which assorted alibi seemed to square things until, to my horror, the papers came out with the story and the picture of me with a newspaper over my head. For several days things at home were disquieting.

So I don't sing much in restaurants any more. Nor put my trust in friends who boast about their Power.

It is quite possible that the restaurant keeper was a good critic and was justified in his violent expression of disapproval. I don't sing well after a heavy dinner. My voice loses power and tightens up on the high notes, and on the day of a performance I never eat much until after I have sung.

The problem of what to do about people who say, "Come to dinner and bring your music," is a more serious one than you would imagine.

Whether my voice is right or not, I love to stand up and let go, but usually, unless I am among very close friends, I try to beg off.

There was a time when I eagerly sought opportunities to sing for my supper. I wanted experience in singing before people, and sometimes these were the only audiences I could get. Often I used to invite a lot of people out to the house and made *them* pay for their dinner by listening to me.

A great many invitations come from persons I have never seen, or whom I have met casually, and whose only interest in me is that they think they might persuade me to put on a show for nothing. These I reject promptly.

Fritz Kreisler was once asked by a rich dowager to come to dinner and bring his violin.

"Really," he said, "you are too kind. There will be no need for me to bring my violin."

"Why not?"

"It doesn't eat," he said.

Some time ago an experience in San Francisco put an end to my after-dinner singing. I sang at a party there one night, and cracked on a high note. The next day the news was all over town that Tibbett was through. How such news travels I don't know, but my agents in New York heard it a week later. I began to get letters from friends in Atlanta and New Orleans, and Minneapolis and Seattle and Wichita, Kans., telling me how sorry they were to hear that my voice was gone! It was a year or more before I stopped running into the rumor. It jeopardized professional engagements, and got me an offer from a musical comedy producer who said that since he heard I was done as an opera singer he thought I might like to try a show for him. He'd have the music written, he promised, without any high notes in it!

Since then I have been careful to refuse stubbornly to sing after heavy dinners.

[43]

When I was in the movies there was a sacred spot on one of the old stages. It was the place where, when I was a struggling youngster, Rupert Hughes introduced me to Mary Garden.

In my early days, the Chicago Opera Company came to Los Angeles every year, and when they sang at the Auditorium I got in for nothing by working as an usher.

In the company were such famous singers as Mary Garden, Muratore, Claudia Muzio, and Baklanoff. I envied them, of course, as a street urchin envies a king, but position such as they held seemed to be so obviously out of my reach that at no time did I have the audacity to hope I might eventually be like them.

At the time I first heard Mary Garden, Rupert Hughes was directing *The Old Nest* at one of the picture studios and asked me if I should like to meet her. He said she was going to visit the studio the next day and that he would introduce me. If I asked her nicely, he said, she might consent to hear me sing.

I floated to the studio. I gulped that I was glad to meet her and, choking, stuttered a request that she let me sing for her. She indicated that she would be delighted to hear me, and told me to telephone her at her hotel the following afternoon for an appointment.

I rushed out to tell all my friends that I was going to sing for Mary Garden! Nobody believed me.

I telephoned her secretary the next day. She had heard nothing about making an appointment with anybody named Tibbett. No, I couldn't speak with Miss Garden; good-by!

I was crushed, angry, disillusioned. My goddess came tumbling down from her temple. To me, then, she was conceited, cruel, and selfish.

And it did not help when my friends asked, "What did Mary Garden say about your voice?"

It was years before I understood that an opera singer cannot possibly listen to all the singers who want an audition. I was only one of a hundred who wanted to sing for her. And had she listened to me, there was nothing much that she could have done except, perhaps, to say that I wasn't as bad as most singers. Probably the day I called was the day of a performance and, as all singers must do, she had shut herself in to rest and practice.

Profiting, however, from that experience, I have always tried to listen to as many young singers as possible. It can't be done on the day of a performance, but when I have a day to spare in a city I listen to as many as time permits. Out of the hundreds that I have heard not many have had voices of promise. Many, when I advised them to give up their ambition for a career, were quite angry with me.

Twice, through no fault of mine, I have had to break my promise to hear young singers. I know they were hurt, as I was hurt when Mary Garden broke her promise to me. I felt worse about it than they did and I wrote them trying to explain, but I'm sure they will never forgive me. At least, not until they rise in their profession and pardon me, as I, understanding at last, pardoned Mary Garden.

A few years ago, when I was singing in a Western city, a woman, well past thirty, came to me with her father, a traveling evangelist. She had a beautiful native voice; she sang accurately and naturally but with absolutely no feeling. Once there had been a great voice in that throat, no doubt about that. Properly trained, as a girl, she might have developed into one of our finest American singers.

After she sang for me she asked whether I would advise her to go to New York to study. She had some money of her own now, she said, looking defiantly at her father.

It was too late to save her voice and, as kindly as possible, I told her so.

"Good," said her father brutally. This man who had announced that he was a Representative of God gloated, "I told you he'd say that. And it's better for all concerned. You keep on with me in the Lord's work and don't go gallivantin' around in theater business."

"Singing," the girl said quickly, "singing to people, making them happy, is just as divine as saving souls." She turned to me. "Isn't it, Mr. Tibbett?"

I said that I believed it was.

"Nonsense!" said the evangelist.

Then it came out that she and her father were at war because he had forced her to give up her voice to revival singing. Since youth she had wanted to leave him to study, but sullenly had obeyed his command that she stay with him to help save souls.

He took her by the arm and led her away. She said not a word but looked back at me with despairing eyes that still haunt me. It was as if I had condemned an innocent woman to life imprisonment.

I wish that I had lied and told her to go.

In introducing me to Mary Garden, Rupert Hughes was performing only one of many kindly acts. Over and over again he helped me enormously. He is best known as a writer, but is a talented musician as well. He plays the piano with professional skill and has composed a number of beautiful songs, many of which I have sung in concerts.

The Ebell Club, a women's organization, brought us together. Hughes was to talk on music before the Club and as part of the program was to present some of his songs. Some of the club members suggested that I do the singing, and I went to see him. Quite frightened in the presence of this famous man, I sang for him. He played the accompaniment, and when we finished he leaned back and looked at me and said, "You have one of the most beautiful voices I have ever heard."

I was greatly pleased, of course, especially because I got the job. I took it for granted that after I sang at the Ebell Club, Rupert Hughes would forget all about me. I was astonished, therefore, when he invited my wife and me to dinner at his home.

At dinner he asked, "What do you intend to do with your life?"

I didn't exactly know. There didn't seem to be much money in singing, so I had thought I might become an orchestral conductor, a position which not only paid well but was highly honored and was a thrilling artistic expression. I had bought a book on conducting and had practiced for hours in front of a mirror, leading a phonograph like nobody's business.

"You have a career in that voice," Hughes said. "You ought to go to New York."

I had heard so many dreadful singers praised that I had learned to scoff at compliments. But I realized that Hughes was no flatterer and that he knew music.

"Lord!" I said to myself. "What if he's right!"

"New York?" I asked aloud. "In order to amount to anything I'd have to study in Europe, wouldn't I? And if Europe were as close as Catalina Island I wouldn't have enough money to get there."

"New York," Hughes said firmly, "is the music center of the world. American singers will soon come into their own and a foreign reputation won't mean a thing. Borrow the money. Some day, with that voice, you'll be able to pay it back."

I thought about it for a week, and then went to James G. Warren, a wealthy business man and one of the kindest, most lovable gentlemen I ever knew. He was president of the Orpheus Club, a men's choral organization in Los Angeles to which I had belonged for several years.

When I told him timidly what I wanted to do he said he would be glad to help. A few weeks later, when I was ready to go, he wrote a check for $2,500, which was the first of many loans through which he helped support me and my family during the critical years. I took out life insurance policies that would pay him back if I died, but that was all the security I could give.

I was twenty-four years old. I promised Mr. Warren and myself that if I hadn't achieved something by the time I was thirty, I would return to Los Angeles and sell trucks for a friend who told me he would give me a job whenever I forgot this singing nonsense and decided to go into a respectable business.

Mr. Warren said he would send me to Frank La Forge in New York, with whom Mr. Warren's daughter, Eleanor, was studying. La Forge was coaching Frances Alda and accompanying Matzenauer and other famous singers in concert work.

In an effort to raise more money, I gave a farewell concert in the Gamut Club auditorium. Rupert Hughes not only accompanied me when I sang a group of his songs, but bought $300 worth of tickets, using only four of them. About 150 persons came to hear me in the auditorium that seated 800. I made $375 on the concert.

Bearing letters of introduction from Rupert Hughes and Mr. Warren, I left my family in Los Angeles and set out to make my fortune. Except for my trips during the war, it was the first time I had ever been outside the state of California, and I was scared to death. I was thrilled, too. Ahead of me was adventure in a great city!

For the first year, however, my adventure was confined mostly to singing in the North Avenue Presbyterian Church in New Rochelle, N. Y., for $75 a month.

I began paying Frank La Forge $12.50 for a half-hour lesson twice a week, and spent $2.20 twice a week for standing room at the Metropolitan Opera House, but soon realized that at that rate my money would quickly vanish. I gave up the opera except on rare occasions, and La Forge, who had taken a real interest in my voice, agreed generously to help me get concert engagements, by means of which I could pay for my lessons.

I was even more fortunate than I realized in being in the hands of a real teacher. I escaped being caught in the singing-teacher racket, which is one of America's greatest fakes. Probably in no profession are there so many incompetent instructors as in music. All over the world they are obtaining money under false pretenses, wasting the time, often actually ruining the careers of potentially successful singers.

They feed their pupils impressive bunk. They say your top notes should come from the bottom—that you sing them from the base of your spine. Others tell you the high notes should come out of the top of your skull. Some teach the singer to pull his tongue back in his throat, or to leave it flat in his mouth. They tear apart the simple art and tell pupils to use this muscle, then that.

Singing is a natural process, as natural as speaking, and a teacher who tries to make a pupil produce tones by thinking only of muscles and chords is as incompetent as an athletic coach who expects to make a man win a 100-yard dash by yelling at him, "Now wiggle the right calf muscle! Now push with your left toe!"

Bad teaching, of course, is worse than no teaching, and there are times when I believe that the person with the average voice who studies with the average teacher may progress farther if he has no instruction at all. Go to Sunday school and listen to the kids sing, and you will learn more in an hour than a great many instructors can give you in a lifetime.

About the only way to tell a bad teacher from a good one is through your own common sense. If he makes singing a mysterious process, if he begins to deal in hocus-pocus, quit him.

One day, after I had been studying about six months with La Forge, like a thunderbolt he said, "I think you ought to try an audition at the Metropolitan."

I was flabbergasted. "I don't know any language but English," I protested. "I don't know any rôles and, besides, my voice isn't big enough for the Metropolitan."

"There's no harm in trying," he said.

The auditions were to be held in April, three months away. We started to work on arias—Iago's *Credo* from *Othello*, Valentine's aria from *Faust*, and *Eri tu* from Verdi's *The Masked Ball*. The aria I sang best, I thought, was the prologue from *Pagliacci*—which I have sung in public more than a thousand times—but that's what every baritone wants to sing, and La Forge said we'd try to use it but he was afraid the judges at the Met wouldn't stand for it.

La Forge made arrangements for the audition, and finally the day arrived. We walked out on the stage. Out of the dark auditorium came a voice: "What will he sing?"

La Forge, at the piano where he was to play my accompaniment, cleared his throat and said hopefully, "The prologue from *Pagliacci*."

"Didn't he bring anything else?" said the voice wearily.

We had lost our first battle. La Forge put the music for the prologue aside and opened *Eri tu*.

In the beginning there is a high F sharp. My voice cracked on it. My knees were shaking as I struggled through the aria.

"Sing something else," the voice said.

I sang Valentine's aria from *Faust*.

"Thank you," came from the blackness of the auditorium.

So we went home and waited for the Metropolitan to send for me.

We waited three weeks, and finally La Forge telephoned Madame Alda for help. She told him to bring me over, and in her apartment I sang for her.

"Pretty tight on top," said Alda, "but a good voice. I'll phone Gatti."

Gatti-Casazza, general director of the Metropolitan, was then her husband.

Gatti didn't remember anything about my audition, but on Alda's recommendation said he would hear me again.

At the second Metropolitan audition I sang Iago's *Credo* from *Othello*. When I finished, that spooky voice asked me to wait.

They offered me $50 a week, for 22 weeks. Before I made my decision, La Forge called Alda and told her about it.

"It's not enough," she said, "for a man with a good voice and a wife and two children to support. I'll phone Gatti."

She called back. "It's all right now," she said triumphantly. "They'll pay you sixty."

I signed a contract—one of those option affairs by which, if they chose, they could keep me for four years, at $100 a week for the second season, $125 for the third, and $150 for the fourth. The contract tied me up tight. I could sing in concerts but, without the Metropolitan's permission, no radio, no musical comedy, no movies. Years later, when I appeared in the movies, I had to pay the Metropolitan a percentage of my earnings.

I noted another strange clause in the standard operatic contract. I was forbidden to wear a hat or to carry a cane at rehearsals. I was to learn later that Gatti had inserted that rule in all contracts because opera singers had turned rehearsals into formal social events and appeared in high collars, silk hats, frock coats, spats, and gold-headed canes and, all dressed up, merely walked through their parts. He made them report in old clothes so they would loosen up and work.

I left Gatti's office with some assurance that I was under way with my career. At twenty-nine, if the Metropolitan took up the options, I would be making $150 a week for twenty-two weeks out of the year. Perhaps I wouldn't have to sell trucks, after all.

As we crossed the dark stage after leaving Gatti's office, a man smiled and bowed to me. "I heard your audition the other day," he said. "May I compliment you on the way you sang the *Credo*. Iago is an old rôle of mine."

I stammered my thanks, and as we left the opera house, I asked La Forge, "Who is that man?"

"That's Scotti," said La Forge, and I almost swooned.

Antonio Scotti, who retired last January at the age of sixty-four, became one of my good friends at the Metropolitan. He was a real actor, and had no use for opera singers who played blatantly to the audience.

"Imagine that the stage is a four-walled room," he told me once. "Keep your face to the audience when the action permits it, but don't be afraid to turn and sing to the back drop. You're performing a play, not singing a concert."

It was in May, 1923, that Scotti so generously praised me, a rank beginner. In January, 1925, on that same stage, I was to experience the greatest moment of my life, in a performance that had been arranged to glorify Scotti, and overnight to find myself turned from an unknown into a Metropolitan star!

Falstaff had been revived as a tribute to Scotti. In the grand revival were Alda, Gigli, Bori, and Kathleen Howard. I was cast as Ford, a secondary rôle.

I got the rôle because Vincente Ballester, the Spanish baritone, who died a few years later, became ill. It was the old, old story of the understudy who gets a chance to make good.

In rehearsal, surrounded by a horde of the greatest names in grand opera, I was at first a stumbling incompetent. I balled up stage directions which, in Italian, had to be translated for me. At one time I was so bad that somebody went to Gatti and said I would never do. Gatti came down to the stage, watched me rehearse, and then talked with Tullio Serafin, the conductor, who had put me in the rôle and was coaching me. Serafin believed in me, and it was only his protest that kept Gatti from throwing me out.

At first I seemed to upset everybody's disposition, and most of the time I was apologizing for some outlandish error that held up the rehearsal.

Other members of the cast were making mistakes, but they laughed them off and nobody seemed to complain. After three of the five weeks of rehearsal were past I discovered a great truth about human nature. If you admit your weaknesses, if you continually apologize, people instinctively scold you—whether it is at a Metropolitan rehearsal or at a contract bridge table. If you never confess your sense of inferiority, if you airily wave aside your errors as if they amounted to nothing, people sneer at you not at all.

I stopped apologizing. Instead of moaning at a stupid error. I merely grinned and shrugged my shoulders. No longer did the stars bark at me. I began to get the hang of the part, and made up my mind to do or die.

The night of the opera I set myself and let go with all I had. In my aria in the second act I tore my heart out. Some subconscious force lifted me up, cleared my throat, and my voice was never better. It is the scene where Ford learns that his wife has been untrue to him and is in love with Falstaff. I went through the scene with terrific desperation, power, and abandon. When I finished I knew that in my furious effort to make the audience pay some attention to me, I had acted the scene well and had sung, for me, superbly.

Marion Telva, who played Dame Quickly, Scotti, and I took a bow. The applause shook the opera house. Then Scotti took a bow alone. Then the three of us again. Then Scotti and I. Then Scotti alone. The applause did not die down.

At last I went to my dressing-room, two flights up, powdered my perspiring face, and came down for the next scene. The applause was holding up the performance. I stood in the wings watching Scotti with envy, hoping that some day I might merit such acclaim. A man came running to me.

"Maestro Serafin," he said, "wants you to take a curtain call alone. The audience is calling for you!"

"For me?" I said. I looked at Gatti, who was standing in the wings across the stage, back of the curtain. He waved me toward the center of the stage. "They want you, not Scotti!" he called. As I walked toward the opening, through the curtain came muffled cries from the audience. At first I couldn't believe my ears.

"Tibbett! Tibbett!" they were crying. "Bravo, Tibbett!"

Alone I stepped out in front of that audience, the audience that had come to cheer Scotti. A thundering wave of applause and cheers smashed me in the face. I almost fainted. I still get goose flesh all over my body when I think of it. Thirty-five hundred persons had their eyes on me. They were cheering *me!* Not Scotti, nor Alda, nor Bori, nor Gigli, nor Kathleen Howard, but ME! There's no thrill in all the world like that!

After the performance Mrs. Tibbett, La Forge, and I went over to a restaurant and had some soup.

"I think you'll get some pretty good notices," La Forge said.

"I hope they do more than to say I was 'adequate,'" I said, and treated myself to another bowl of soup.

I still didn't realize what had happened. The next morning my wife woke me up by shouting excitedly, "The hall outside is full of reporters and photographers! Look at the papers! On the *front page!* You were the hit of the performance!"

Then I believed in Santa Claus!

Escamillo in *Carmen*

Valentin in *Faust*

Rigoletto

In the MGM movie *The Rogue Song*

In the title role of *The Emperor Jones*

Scarpia in *Tosca*

Wolfram in *Tännhauser*

War Memorial Opera House

FRIDAY EVENING, APRIL 26, 1935, at 8:30

Only San Francisco Concert

Tickets at Sherman, Clay Co., San Francisco and Oakland

CONLEY MANAGEMENT

TIBBETT

Student Concert Managers John C. Collins, William R. Moran
and Elinor Hall with Lawrence Tibbett after a Stanford University
Memorial Auditorium concert, January 24, 1940

Don Carlos in *La Forza del Destino*

Lawrence Tibbett and Catherine Dale Owen in the
MGM movie *The Rogue Song*, 1930

In *The Rogue Song*

Lawrence Tibbett in his many roles

Rigoletto

In the title role of *Simone Boccanegra*

Michele in *Il Tabarro*

THE WORLD OF MUSIC
applauds
LAWRENCE TIBBETT

BUFFALO
The occasion took on gala aspects—auditorium and extra stage seats filled with eager Tibbett admirers. —*Buffalo News.*

COLUMBUS
The walls of Memorial Hall fairly bulged with the press of people that managed to find room inside to hear the most versatile of present-day singers. —*Columbus Citizen.*

DETROIT
An enthusiastic audience of such proportion that it filled the auditorium of Masonic Temple and overflowed onto the stage. —*Detroit Free Press.*

LOS ANGELES
When Tibbett sings packed houses are an invariable rule, and last night they packed them in on the stage and even on chairs in the aisles until the auditorium would hold no more. —*Los Angeles News.*

Herbert Graf rehearsing *La Forza del Destino* with
Frederick Jagel, Zinka Milanov, Ezio Pinza and Lawrence Tibbett

Grace Moore, Lucrezia Bori and Lawrence Tibbett
with the Metropolitan Board's George Sloan

Lawrence Tibbett and Kirsten Flagstad

IV

WHY I QUIT MAKING FUNNY FACES

WHEN I went to Hollywood in 1929 to make my first motion picture, *The Rogue Song*, it was against the violent protest of most of my friends. They said the movies were a thing depraved and that I had become money-crazy and was wrecking my career for gold.

I disarmed my advisers somewhat by confessing that perhaps I was money-crazy. I owed a good many thousands of dollars to friends who had financed my career, and here was a chance to pay back every dollar. If that is being money-crazy, so be it.

The Metropolitan Opera Company was then engaging me for twenty-two weeks out of the year. I was making some money on concerts and from phonograph records. I had been fortunate in turning out a good record of the Prologue from *Pagliacci*, and the royalties the first year had totaled nearly $10,000.

It might seem to the public that I should have been rolling in wealth, but most of an opera singer's money goes for commissions to managers, musical coaching, traveling expenses, accompanists, wigs, advertising, entertaining, pianos, music, and heaven knows what else.

The movies offered me a great deal of money, and I accepted. Some of my colleagues at the Metropolitan as well as some of the newspaper critics predicted that I would be ruined as an artist.

"Look here," I said, irritated by their smugness; "I believe that the best actors in the world are in the movies. No less an artist than Lionel Barrymore is going to direct my first picture. When I come back here, thanks to the movies, I hope to be a better artist than I am now."

"Poor Tibbett," they said. "He's already gone Hollywood! His operatic career is ended!"

Last January, at the première of the opera, *The Emperor Jones*, the critics and the audience were enthusiastic. They gave me twenty-two curtain calls.

Eugene O'Neill's powerful and unique play, set to music by Louis Gruenberg, is almost a monologue for the Emperor. The lines are spoken on the music and it is primarily an acting part, as the cocksure, bullying Pullman porter turns into a terror-stricken, whining fugitive. Whatever success I had in acting that part was greatly enhanced by the lessons I learned in Hollywood.

I must admit that when I first went to work in a motion picture studio, I began to wonder if things were going to come out all right, after all. The first voice tests were not so good. I sang so loud that I blew out a light valve in the recording apparatus. I have no idea what a light valve may be, but, after I finished a song, people began running around yelling excitedly and telephoning for help, and when I asked what it was all about they said accusingly, "You blew out a light valve!" I shrank into a corner, afraid to ask what a light valve was, for fear I should learn that I had caused damage amounting to thousands of dollars and that they were going to make me pay for it. I learned later that, whatever it is, it costs about $45.

We got the sound straightened out, but the camera tests and the make-up almost caused me to run down to the ocean and drown myself in shame. They had to learn how to light me. They studied both sides of my face, from all angles and altitudes. I stood on a stage, while a dozen men and women, frowning and muttering, looked me over as though I were a horse. Electricians fussed with lights, cameramen held their hands in front of their faces and glared at me through spread-out fingers, now eying me from the floor, now from a perch on a chair, to see whether there was any way to shoot this guy so he'd look somewhat human.

They advised me to grow a mustache, which I started at once and found that the hair grew luxuriantly on the left side of my lip but hardly at all on the right. They fixed that by patching in some false hair. Eventually the right side caught up and I was able to abandon the false half-mustache.

They said all leading men must have wavy hair, and sent me to a hairdresser for a permanent wave! I made the appointment for very late at night and stole into the hairdresser's through a side door so no one would see me, and sat for hours with my hair wrapped around those diabolical hot electric gadgets. I was ashamed to go around Hollywood dolled up in such a manner, and whenever I had my hat off I expected at any moment to be mistaken for Mary Pickford.

They said my ears stuck out too much, and pasted them down with glue and tape.

It was all new to me, and I took orders without protesting until I went on the stage for my first scene. Lines were marked on the stage, showing me where to stand and where not to walk. My hair was curled, I wore half a false mustache, my ears were pasted back. It was a hot day; the picture was being made in color and the batteries of lights were like an open furnace. I was bundled up in a Russian costume meant for sleighing in Siberia. I had learned my lines for the first scene.

"What do you want me to do?" I asked Lionel Barrymore.

"Just act natural," he said.

Act *natural!* Under those circumstances!

"Just be yourself," he said.

"O. K.!" I said. I tore off the Russian fur hat and slammed it on the floor. I started to unbutton the coat. I saw then that Lionel was grinning at me.

"That disrobing scene, Mr. Tibbett," he drawled, "doesn't come until later in the picture. If you don't mind, we'll shoot the scenes in their proper order."

I stopped short. Then I laughed. He laughed. Everybody on the stage laughed. I put on the fur hat and started to work. I believe that is the only time in my life that I ever exhibited any of that much-talked-of and seldom-seen emotion called operatic temperament.

It wasn't long before I became accustomed to all my make-up. I had only one mishap. After *The Prodigal* was finished, when executives were looking at it in the projection-room, one suddenly shouted, "Look! His ear!" They looked. In the midst of a love scene, my right ear suddenly popped out like a swinging door. The glue had let go, and up to that time no one had noticed it. I thought it was a quite interesting magical effect—an ear coming out of nowhere—but they made me do the scene over again.

I had been in Hollywood only a few weeks when I engaged my first man-servant. He was a distinguished-looking young man with a foreign accent, and he acted as my dresser and valet at the studio and occasionally helped serve dinner at home.

A week after I had engaged him I discovered he was a Russian count —a real one, according to other refugee Russians in Hollywood. It didn't seem right for a real count to be pressing my pants, and I told him so. He said he needed the money and was very happy to work for me.

I protested: "When you are around here, you mustn't act so much like a menial. Though you are working for me, I'd rather have you consider yourself somewhat as one of the family."

He thanked me and said he would.

That evening I had a number of guests, and after dinner they wandered out into the garden. After a while Elsie Janis, the actress, came up to me and said, "What's the matter with this butler of yours? He just asked me to take a drive with him down to the beach!"

A moment later Helen Wills Moody, the tennis champion, said my butler had invited her to play tennis with him the next day, and Basil Rathbone, the actor, told me he hoped he hadn't hurt my feelings, but he had just turned down my butler's suggestion that the party was getting dull and that they ought to start a bridge game.

I explained to the count that while I did not want him to act exactly like a menial, I had not intended that he promote himself to co-host. He became quite abusive and said that he didn't think much of me and my guests, anyway, so we parted company.

Although I had grown up in Los Angeles, I didn't know much about life in a movie studio. I took things as they came and made no complaint. Other stars said I was foolish because I didn't go around demanding things. You weren't respected, they said, unless you demanded things.

"What things?" I asked. "I have everything I want."

"Make them give you a better dressing-room. Ask for John Gilbert's."

My dressing-room was all right—much better than anything I ever had at the Metropolitan—but just as a try-out I went into the front office and demanded John Gilbert's dressing-room. It was not in use at that time.

I got it at once.

"How long," I asked myself, "has this been going on? Just ask, and you get!"

I made up my mind that if the way to become respected on a movie lot was to ask for things, I'd build myself into a god. But after I got the dressing-room, I sat and sat and thought and thought but never could think of another thing to ask for, so I guess I wasn't respected very much.

When I finished *The Rogue Song*, one of the officials told me, "We're suppressing in our advertising the fact that you're an opera singer. I hope it won't hurt your feelings."

It didn't hurt my feelings particularly, but it aroused my curiosity.

"You hired me because I sang at the Metropolitan, didn't you?" I asked.

"Yes."

"Then what's the idea?"

"There's a curse on opera singers," he said. "Caruso made a couple of pictures years ago, and the first one was such a flop that they never released the second."

"That was a silent picture," I said. "And, anyway, didn't Geraldine Farrar do well in the movies?"

"She was a woman. That's different. Men opera singers"—he held up his hands—"no good. The movie fans think they're fat and speak in a foreign language and smell of garlic. We'll bill you as a new singing star and forget the Metropolitan."

The Rogue Song played for five months at the Astor Theater in New York, and I was advertised there as a Metropolitan Opera star. But in all other theaters throughout the country my supposedly shameful connection with grand opera was carefully suppressed. Laurel and Hardy were in *The Rogue Song* and at that time had not reached anywhere near their present popularity. Any conceit that I might have had regarding my box office value as a movie star was quickly eliminated when, passing through a small Western town on a train, I saw on a theater canopy: "Laurel and Hardy in *The Rogue Song.*"

It was not until I had made two motion pictures that theater officials generally looked upon me as a star and advertised my name without much reluctance.

The movies began to improve my acting the minute I saw the shots of the first scenes. To my utter astonishment I discovered that every time I took a high note I looked at the end of my nose and crossed my eyes! I was twisting my mouth into queer shapes, and when I pronounced certain words they didn't sound at all the way I expected.

I was using Operatic Gesture No. 1—the right hand above the heart, the left hand extended skyward—to mean anything! I used it for "I love you very much," "It looks like rain," "Good night, Mother," and "No, I don't believe I'll have any more spinach."

I learned that action is not necessarily acting. Lionel Barrymore taught me to *think* of an emotion and to use only enough gestures to get the idea over. He knocked out of me forever, I hope, almost everything I had learned to imitate in bad operatic acting of the old school.

I believe that the secret of Greta Garbo's success as an actress lies in the fact that she can stay still and concentrate on an idea, and hold your interest, longer than any other actor I ever saw.

I lied when *Who's Who in America* first asked me for biographical data. I said that I made my opera première at the Metropolitan as Valentine in *Faust*. I was loath to confess that I had made so little impression on the operatic powers that they launched me in what is probably the most insignificant rôle in opera.

I played one of two monks in *Boris Godunov*. We sang about twenty bars of music in Latin, most of it off-stage. I didn't even put on make-up. We walked on the stage, were pelted with stones by a mob, and retreated. Then we took off our monks' costumes and went home.

Unimportant though it was, I was well satisfied. I was quite proud to have started my career with Chaliapin, who sang Boris. Chaliapin, I believe, is the greatest operatic performer we have ever had. His was a magnificent personality and he was the strongest single influence in bringing to the operatic stage real acting, as opposed to operatic acting.

As Chaliapin tops the singing actors, so does John McCormack lead in his line. McCormack is my favorite concert singer and he is a good friend of mine.

Several years ago at the Bohemian Grove, near San Francisco, John and I got into a friendly argument as to the merits of our respective B flats.

"I can sing a better B flat than you can," I said, and produced a sample.

"Maybe so," he grinned, "but I get more money for my B flats than you do."

Which ended the argument.

My performance of Valentine was my second appearance at the Metropolitan. Three days before the performance I was notified that because of Vincente Ballester's illness I had been assigned to the rôle. Coached chiefly by Wilfred Pelletier, assistant conductor, working day and night, I learned the part. With the help of the prompter, I got through the opera without serious mishap, but to this day the music of *Faust* makes me catch my breath, and when I make my first entrance over the bridge, as Valentine, my knees shake most deplorably.

After I appeared in *Faust* I was visited by a swarthy man who runs a claque at the Metropolitan. For $25 he guaranteed to deliver at least two bows at any performance.

I asked the Metropolitan officials about it and they told me not to waste my money. It was then that I heard that every opera house has a claque of its own—a body of men and women, spotted in strategic parts of the house, who lead the applause and make sure that it comes at the right time.

A claque cannot rouse an audience that has not been stirred by a performance. But for a worthy performance it can get applause under way. Americans will join in applause but seldom will initiate it. However, an audience quickly resents an obvious effort to stimulate applause and, frowning, sits at once on its hands; so the claque must only suggest and never blatantly lead.

An opera singer cannot live without his bows, which he counts as a kid counts his new agates. There is a technique in bowing to an audience which it took me several years to learn.

Mrs. Paul Cravath, who was Agnes Huntington, a famous singing actress, gave me my first lessons in taking curtain calls.

"You're popping out and in," she said. "Stand still when you get out there. Let them see you! Look at each person in the opera house and make him think you're a good friend of his. And, after you step back, don't wait until they *demand* your presence. When the applause seems to be dying, take another bow!"

Grand opera seems to stir audiences to greater enthusiasm than any other theatrical effort, and, because I had become accustomed to the urge of the audience, when I contracted to sing regularly over the radio I found myself in the most difficult work I had ever attempted.

The inspiration of an audience is a definite physiological stimulant. When I sing to a radio microphone I feel like a football player who is charging through a line in front of empty stands.

I shut my eyes and try to pretend that I am singing to an audience. I act the part that I am singing, and when I finish I try to imagine that somewhere somebody is applauding.

Unless he has had years of radio experience a singer usually suffers instinctively a distinct shock like a slap in the face when his song ends and nothing, *absolutely nothing*, happens! For a moment, until you realize where you are, something clutches at your stomach, and in the deathlike silence you think, "Gosh! Not a sound! Am I as bad as all *that!*"

It is rather disturbing, that twenty-four-hour wait until the mail man comes in with the applause.

The task of choosing songs for the radio audience is a difficult one. Requests are divided rather evenly between popular and classical music, so I attempt to solve the problem by singing a little of every kind.

This was a problem that confronted me when I first sang over the radio—in Los Angeles in 1922. I was honored by being invited to sing for Station KHJ. I worried for days, and finally selected a program of operatic songs that I decided would be worthy of this great occasion. Millions, they told me, would listen in.

I sang, and got along rather well and felt that I must have become famous overnight. The next day I waited for congratulations, but none of my friends had radios and not one had heard me. It was a great shock. I went around asking utter strangers what they thought of Lawrence Tibbett's radio début, and all they said was "Huh?" To this day I have never found even one person—out of the audience of millions that I imagined was listening breathlessly—who heard me over KHJ in 1922.

When I began to sing regularly at the Metropolitan, Rupert

Hughes tried to get me a summer job in opera in Chicago. The impresario told Hughes, "I never heard of him. I couldn't use an unknown."

Two years later this impresario said to Hughes, "I heard Lawrence Tibbett recently. He's great!"

"Why don't you engage him?" Hughes asked.

"He's too expensive. I need a baritone, though. Perhaps I could place that friend of yours. What was his name?"

"Tibbett," said Hughes.

I started at the Metropolitan at a salary of $60 a week. They gave me a bonus of $1,500 for my second season, in which I first did Ford in *Falstaff*, but they raised my salary to only $90 a week, instead of the $100 my contract promised.

My wife and the twins had joined me in New York and the expenses were high. I had practically thrown away $750, which was the cost of giving a recital.

During the first season at the Metropolitan I had a mild attack of influenza and got out of bed to sing with Jeritza in a scene from the last act of *Carmen*. The company was doing a program of big scenes from various operas. I sang Escamillo, the toreador, who has very little to do in that scene. But it was my first year in grand opera, and to appear as the toreador with Jeritza in any scene at all from *Carmen* seemed to be an opportunity for which I could justifiably risk my life.

The day after the performance I had a relapse and went to a hospital, where they said I had spinal meningitis. They were wrong, but I wasn't back at the Metropolitan for three weeks. Rupert Hughes happened to be in New York and came to see me. I was broke, and he lent me $300 to pay my hospital bill. Luckily, I have never been ill since then.

I was fortunate that the Metropolitan kept me, and thus gave me the opportunity, in my second season, to sing Ford. At the end of my first twenty-two weeks they told me that they didn't want me particularly and offered me $75, instead of the $100 that the option called for. After my tearful protests, they raised it to $90, which I accepted. It was then that I learned what "option" means. I was so inexperienced in legal language that I had thought I had a four-year contract at certain definite figures. I discovered that the Metropolitan had an option to do with me about as they chose. The only option I had was to take it or leave it.

They had an idea that my health was bad, and at the Metropolitan they don't want singers who are likely to become ill just before a performance.

The newspaper publicity that I received for the *Falstaff* performance started a rumor that the Metropolitan had raised my salary to fabulous figures. There were other stories, to the effect that I was to take Scotti's place immediately, that Scotti and I were at swords' points, that he was jealous of me. Newspapers said he had tried to prevent me from taking a bow when the audience applauded for me.

When these stories appeared, Scotti came to me and said, "I hope you realize that I wouldn't do anything like that." And certainly in the enthusiasm and excitement of the moment neither Scotti nor I had realized the situation.

A few weeks later, when I was singing at the Metropolitan, William M. Sullivan, my attorney, sat in a box with, among others, Mrs. Lawrence Townsend, a distinguished patron of music and wife of the former ambassador to Belgium, and Rufus L. Patterson, the tobacco man. Patterson said, "After his success in *Falstaff* I suppose Tibbett's troubles are over. The Metropolitan must be paying him a large salary now."

Sullivan told him how much I was getting.

"That's a shame," Patterson said. "We'll have to do something about that."

Unknown to me, Sullivan had already discussed with Mrs. Townsend the fact that my income did not in any way meet my expenses. When Patterson offered to help, Mrs. Townsend and Sullivan organized themselves into an informal committee, and a few days later they received nearly $4,000.

Among the contributors were Mr. Patterson, Mrs. Ida A. Polk, Mrs. Charles B. Alexander, Mrs. Marius DeBrabant, Mrs. William Crocker, Mrs. Charles E. Mitchell, and Clarence Mackay. It was their tribute to a young American artist, they said, not a loan. I insisted upon accepting it as a loan, or having the privilege of repaying my debt of gratitude by singing at their homes.

When I sang *The King's Henchman*, at its première in January, 1927, I first *felt* the strong concentration of an audience on the story. Edna St. Vincent Millay wrote the libretto and Deems Taylor the music. It was the first time I ever sang in English at the Metropolitan, and at the end of the performance, I made up my mind that I would crusade actively all my life for opera in English.

Edna St. Vincent Millay wrote a beautiful and singable libretto for *The King's Henchman*, though some of the patrons of the opera were shocked when the Henchman sang right out in English a complaint that his feet hurt him.

Miss Millay is a tiny, brilliant, energetic person and in rehearsals won a battle from the entire staff of the Metropolitan Opera Company. The opera ran a little long, and the conductor and stage manager decided to cut out my last aria. Deems Taylor protested, but finally gave up. I said I thought they were all wrong, then was forced to surrender.

So they cut out the aria.

Miss Millay came to a rehearsal the next day and missed the aria. Taylor told her what had happened.

She gritted her teeth. "They won't cut that out of *my* opera!" she declared.

The Metropolitan staff had conquered many a woman opera singer, but never before had gone into battle with a poetess. I could have told them something about the futility of arguing with a poetess! For the first time in the history of the opera a woman had the maestros scared to death.

"That is the best scene in the opera. If it goes out," she said, "the entire opera goes out. We stop right now!" And they knew that she meant it.

The aria stayed in. And she was right. It turned out to be the peak of the performance. . . .

And now I come to the most important event in my life—my second marriage, which brought me quiet, sympathy, inspiration, and companionship such as I had dreamed of, but which I thought actually existed only in those vague promises of Hans Christian Andersen: "And so they lived happily ever after."

It was in San Francisco that I met the present Mrs. Lawrence Tibbett. I had gone to a reception to meet Herbert Hoover, then Secretary of Commerce, who was the guest of honor at the home of George T. Cameron, owner of the *San Francisco Chronicle*. I was in San Francisco for a holiday at the Bohemian Grove, where, during my vacation, I sang *St. Francis of Assisi*.

At the reception I was asked to sing, and I did, gladly. After a number of encores I felt that I had given my voice all the use it should have that evening and decided that neither wild horses nor Herbert Hoover could make me sing again. Then a lovely lady approached me. She had read of my success as Ford in *Falstaff*, she said. She had followed my career through the newspapers. Wouldn't I please— And I found myself singing her favorite song, *Drink to Me Only with Thine Eyes*.

She was Mrs. Jennie Marston Burgard, a New York girl, living in San Francisco, the daughter of Edgar L. Marston, a retired banker. She knew music, was fond of the opera, and we instantly became good friends.

On January 1, 1932, the year after my first marriage was dissolved, we were married. Our son was born in August of this year. Because we agree that the life of a successful artist is the happiest of all, combining as it does avocation and vocation, we shall do everything possible to develop his interest in the arts.

Since our marriage, ours has been a tranquil life, born of complete understanding. My wife is interested most in my career, and we like to do things together, whether it is a motoring trip in Europe or a midnight jaunt to Harlem. Whenever possible, she travels with me on tour, and is at the opera every night that I sing and usually is the first to greet me in my dressing-room after a performance.

We avoid as far as possible elaborate social functions. We are not hermits, but we do enjoy each other best and we have more fun sitting quietly at home, discussing intensely and at great length what probably to most people would seem to be quite trivial subjects, than we would have at a formal dinner party where men and women debate the affairs of the nation.

My wife has a fine mind, a marvelous sense of humor, and a sound feminine instinct which saves me from many a blunder. Like me, she abhors sham and pretense, and, as much as my life will permit, we try to live the sane, happy, normal life of two newlyweds in an average social circle in the average American city. I feel quite sure that our honeymoon will never end.

Many men, I think, all their lives dream of an ideal princess. For some the dream never becomes a reality, the princess is always far away, just out of their grasp. To those men the promise of a happy life is only half fulfilled. I am extremely fortunate in that, beyond the shadow of a doubt, my dream has come true. Like the two in the opera—here is my Isolde. . . .

As I write this, the Metropolitan is about to start another season, cut from a brave twenty-four to a pitiful fourteen weeks. Philadelphia and Chicago, once great opera centers, have practically given up the ghost.

I love opera. It is the most extravagant and idealistic gesture that man has made in the theater. But opera as it is today, I am afraid, cannot survive.

Opera must take off its high hat. It must present its librettos in English, and those librettos must be sung by artists who have learned to enunciate the English language so that it can be understood—which is as we speak it, simply and naturally.

It is too much a spectacle. Opera houses are too large for a keen emotional contact between the audience and the actors.

The opera is suffering from tradition. The long gray beards are tripping it up. It needs a housecleaning and some showmanship. It is still trying to make the people adapt themselves to the old-fashioned opera, instead of adapting the opera to the modern-day music lover.

The whole structure of opera must be Americanized if Americans are to support it in the long run.

Most of the old patrons of the opera, themselves, are fed up with its antique art. The rich and the society leaders—no longer quite so rich—who made opera-going the fashionable thing to do, are withdrawing their support. And now that opera needs audiences, it finds that by being snobbish it has alienated the great middle class of music lovers. Even if opera houses should reduce their admission prices to the fees charged for a good musical comedy, which ought to be done immediately, they would have trouble in drawing the crowds.

The Metropolitan needs the patronage of only 3,000 persons at each performance in order to be successful. If 1,500 men and their wives, out of the millions in NewYork and vicinity, decide to go to the opera tonight, they will fill every desirable seat at the Metropolitan and most of those worthless ones, high up, 'way back and against the wall, from which the disgusted and hornswoggled purchaser can see no more of the stage than if he had bought a seat on a barrel up an alley in Hoboken. I know about those seats. They are the ones that were handed to me when I first came to New York.

But those 1,500 couples won't go to the opera tonight, and half the opera house is likely to be empty. The opera's worship of foreign gods and its overaccentuation of the social side has driven to concerts, to the radio, and to musical comedy hundreds of thousands of music lovers who, even with opera as it is now produced, would thoroughly enjoy it.

THE GLORY ROAD

Grand opera today is still truly grand—but fine singing, splendid orchestras, and artistic stagecraft are not enough to bring in the dollars of the average man, whose dollars opera must have in order to survive.

The old fogies, when I argue this, say I am crazy. But I wish some forward-looking impresario would try it. Let him get a great American librettist to translate such classics as *Tristan und Isolde* and *Tosca* and *Carmen* into English. Let him charge not more than $3.30 for the best seat in the house and tour the leading cities of the United States with a company of singers from the Metropolitan, including, I hope (if this insubordination doesn't cause me to lose my job!), Lawrence Tibbett.

Would you be there?

LAWRENCE TIBBETT (1896-1960) - A DISCOGRAPHY

by W. R. Moran

Honorary Curator, Archive of Recorded Sound, Stanford University

I. THE VICTOR RECORDINGS

Discog. No.	Matrix-Take	Date	Victor Cat.No.	HMV Cat.No.	Other	LP Recordings	Speed (rpm)
1.	Die Allmacht (Pyrker, trans. Baker-Schubert, D.852) (E) (Pf. Stewart Wille)						
	CS-046070-1,-2	4 Jan. '40	15891	(DB 5762)		VIC 1340	78.26
*2.	The Bailiff's Daughter (Old English Ballad) (E) (Pf. Stewart Wille)						
	CS-75708-1,-2	28 Mar. '33	-------	-------	-------	-------	
3.	The Bailiff's Daughter (Old English Ballad) (E) (Pf. Stewart Wille)						
	CS-046067-1,-2	4 Jan. '40	15549	-------	-------	CAL 168	78.26
*4.	UN BALLO IN MASCHERA: Eri tu che macchiavi (Verdi) (I) (Or. Nathaniel Shilkret)						
	CVE-53454-1	31 May '29	-------	-------	-------	LM 6705-4 / VIC 1340 / CAL 171	76.60
	-2	15 April'30	7353 / 11-8861	-------	-------	-------	76.60
	-3,-4	15 April '30	7353 / 15819	DB 1478	-------	-------	76.60
*5.	IL BARBIERE DI SIVIGLIA: Largo al factotum (Rossini) (I) (Or. Nathaniel Shilkret)						
	CVE-59753-1	15 April '30	7353	-------	-------	LM 6705-4 / VIC 1340 / CAL 171 / LM 21034	76.60
	-2,-3,-4	15 April '30	7353 / 14202	DB 1478	-------	-------	76.60
6.	IL BARBIERE DI SIVIGLIA: Senti, ma Lindoro...Dunque io son (Rossini) (w. Amelita Galli-Curci) (I) (Or.Bourdon)						
	BVE-35446-1,-2,-3,-4	7 May '26	-------	-------	-------	-------	
7.	Battle Hymn of the Republic (Julia Ward Howe-William Steffe, Orch. by Bruno Reibold) (Or. dir. by Wilfred Pelletier)						
	BS-036848-1,-1A	3 May '39	4433	-------	-------	-------	78.26

* see NOTES at end

8. Believe Me, If All Those Endearing Young Charmes (Thomas Moore) (Hp. Lapitino; Or. Bourdon)
   BVE-37879-1,-2,-3   30 Mar. '27   1238   DA. 886   --------   CAE 158 / CAL 168   76.60

9. Calm as the Night (Carl Goetz) (w. Lucrezia Bori) (Or. Bourdon)
   BVE-28854-1,-2,-3   1 June '27   3043 / 1747   DA 912   --------   77.43

*10. CARMEN: Votre toast! (Chanson du Toréador) (Bizet) (w. Metropolitan Opera Chor. and Orch., conducted by Giulio Setti)
   CVE-51117-1,-2,-3   3 April '29   --------   --------   LM 7605-4 / CAL 171 / CAL 346 / VIC 1340   76.00
   -4   8 April '29   8124   --------   --------   76.00
   -5   8 April '29   8124 / 14202   DB 1298   --------   76.00

CONTES D'HOFFMANN see "Tales of Hoffmann"

11. The Crucifix (Fauré) (E) (w. Richard Crooks) (Organ: Mark Andrews)
   BVE-43720-1,-2,-3   10 April '28   --------   --------   --------
   CVE-43720-1,-2,-3   30 Jan. '29   --------   --------   --------

12. THE CRUCIFIXION: So thou liftest Thy petition (Sir John Stainer) (w. Richard Crooks) (Organ: Mark Andrews)
   BVE-43721-1,-2,-3   10 April '28   --------   --------   --------
   CVE-43721-1,-2,-3   30 Jan. '29   --------   --------   --------

NOTE: [ ] = side numbers within sets

* THE CRUCIFIXION (Oratorio in 12 parts by Sir John Stainer) (w. Richard Crooks, Wilfred Glenn, Frank Croxton & Trinity Choir, dir. Clifford Cairns. Organ: Mark Andrews) (M-64)

13.[1] (a) And they came to a place called Gethsemane (Crooks); (b) Could ye not watch with me one brief hour? (Tibbett)
   CVE-53735-1,-2   27 May '29   9424 / 9430 / 13262   D 1817 / D 7770   CAL 235 / VIC 1403   77.43

14.[2]. (a) And they laid their hands on Him (Crooks, Tibbett, Glenn); (b) Processional to Calvary (Andrews)
CVE-53736-1,-2   27 May '29   D 1817   9424   CAL 235   77.43
                                D 7771   9431   VIC 1403
                                          13262

[3]. Processional to Calvary, pt. 2: Fling wide the Gates (Trinity Choir & Andrews)
CVE-53737-1   27 May '29   D 1818   9425   --------   CAL 235   77.43
                            D 7772   9432   VIC 1403
                                      13263

[4]. Processional to Calvary, pt. 3: How sweet is the Grace (Crooks)
CVE-53738-1,-2   27 May '29   D 1818   9425   CAL 235   77.43
                               D 7773   9433   VIC 1403
                                         13264

15.[5]. (a) And when they were come (Tibbett);   (b) Cross of Jesus (Choir);   (c) He made Himself no reputation
(Tibbett)
CVE-53739-1,-2   27 May '29   D 1819   9426   --------   CAL 235   77.43
                               D 7774   9434   VIC 1403
                                         13265

[6]. King ever Glorious (Crooks)
CVE-53740-1,-2   27 May '29   D 1819   9426   --------   CAL 235   77.43
                               D 7775   9435   VIC 1403
                                         13266

16.[7]. (a) And as Moses lifted up the serpent (Tibbett);   (b) God so loved the world (Choir)
CVE-53741-1,-2   28 May '29   D 1820   9427   --------   CAL 235   77.43
                               D 7775   9430   VIC 1403
                                         13266

17.[8]. (a) Jesus said, "Father forgive them" (Crooks);   (b) So Thou liftest Thy petition (Crooks & Tibbett)
CVE-53742-1   28 May '29   D 1820   9427   --------   CAL 235   77.43
                           D 7774   9431   VIC 1403
                                     13265

18.[9]. (a) Jesus, the crucified (Choir);   (b) And one of the Malefactors (Tibbett, Glenn, Croxton);
(c) I adore Thee (Choir)
CVE-53743-1,-2   28 May '29   D 1821   9428   --------   CAL 235   77.43
                               D 7773   9432   VIC 1403
                                         13264

19.[10]. (a) When Jesus therefore saw his mother (Crooks, Tibbett); (b) Is it nothing to you? (Tibbett)
CVE-53744-1,-2 28 May '29   9428   D 1821   --------   CAL 235
                           9433   D 7772   VIC 1403   77.43
                           13263

[11]. From the throne of His cross, pt. 1 (Choir)
CVE-53745-1,-2 28 May '29   9429   D 1822   --------   CAL 235
                           9434   D.7771   VIC 1403   77.43
                           13262
          -3   29 May '29   --------   --------   --------   --------

[12]. (a) From the throne of His cross, pt. 2 (Choir); (b) After this (Crooks); (c) All for Jesus (Choir)
CVE-53746-1,-2 28 May '29   9429   D 1822   --------   CAL 235
                           9435   D 7770   VIC 1403   77.43
                           13261

*20. THE CUBAN LOVE SONG: Cuban Love Song (from M-G-M film) (Herbert Stothart-Dorothy Fields-Jimmy McHugh)
    (Pf. Stewart Wille)
PBVE-68328-1,-2 28 Oct. '31   1550   DA 1251   --------   --------   78.26

*21. THE CUBAN LOVE SONG: Cuban Love Song (from M-G-M film) (Herbert Stothart-Dorothy Fields-Jimmy McHugh)
    (Or. Nathaniel Shilkret)
BVE-69068-1,-2,-3,-4 10 Dec. '31   (1550: see NOTE)--------   --------   77.43

*22. THE CUBAN LOVE SONG: Cuban Love Song (from M-G-M film) (Herbert Stothart-Dorothy Fields-Jimmy McHugh)
    (Tenor part only. No accompaniment)
BVE-69071-1,-2 12 Dec. '31   1550   --------   --------   CAE 160
                                                    CAL 168   77.43

23. THE CUBAN LOVE SONG: Tramps at Sea (from M-G-M film) (Herbert Stothart-Dorothy Fields-Jimmy McHugh)
    (Pf. Stewart Wille)
PBVE-68327-1,-2,-3 26 Oct. '31   1550   DA 1251   --------   CAL 171   78.26

*24. Drink To Me Only With Thine Eyes (Ben Jonson) (Pf. Roy Shields)
-------- (Test recording) 13 Apr. '25 --------

25. Drink To Me Only With Thine Eyes (Ben Jonson) (Or. Bourdon)
BVE-37878-1,-2,-3 30 Mar. '27   1238   DA 886   --------   CAE 160   76.60

*26. Edward (Herder - Karl Loewe, Op. 1 No. 1) (E) (Pf. Stewart Wille)
PCVE-68333-1,-2 29 Oct. '31   7486   --------   --------   VIC 1340   78.26
CVE-68333-3,-4 12 Dec. '31   7486   DB 1684   --------   --------   77.43

27. EMPEROR JONES: Oh Lord!...Standin' in the need of prayer (Louis Gruenberg, Op. 36) (w. Metropolitan
Opera House Orch., cond. by Wilfred Pelletier)
CS-81087-1   19 Jan. '34   --------   --------   ED 24   LM 6705-4
    -1A,-2,-2A   19 Jan. '34   7959   --------   --------   --------   77.43

28. FALSTAFF: È sogno o realtà? (Ford's Monologue) (Verdi) (I) (Or. Rosario Bourdon)
CVE-34930-1,-2,-3,-4,-5   3 Mar.'26   --------   --------   --------

*29. FAUST: O sainte medaille...Avant de quitter ces lieux (Gounod) (F) (Or. Nathaniel Shilkret)
CS-82331-1,-1A   20 April '34   8452   DB 2262   --------   LM 6705-4
                                                                    VIC 1340
                                                                    CAL 171   77.43

*30. THE FORTUNE TELLER: Gypsy Love Song (Harry B. Smith-Victor Herbert) (Pf. Roy Shields)
-------- (Test recording) 13 Apr.'25   --------   --------   --------

31. De Glory Road (Clement Wood-Jacques Wolfe) (Pf. Stewart Wille)
PCVE-68331-1,-2   29 Oct. '31   --------   --------   --------   CAL 168
CVE-68331-3,-4,-5   10 Dec. '31   7486   DB 1684   --------   --------   77.43

*32. Goin' Home (Williams Arms Fisher, adapted from Largo movement, Dvorak's Symphony "From the New World")
(E) (Or. Alexander Smallens)
CS-02176-1   19 Oct. '36   15549   DB 3036   --------   CAL 168
                                    11-8860   CAE 217   77.43

33. Hallelujah Rhythm (Or. Alexander Smallens)
CS-02175-1,-1A   19 Oct. '36   --------   --------   --------

*34. If Love Hath Entered Thy Heart (Marz) (Pf. Stewart Wille)
BS-75709-1   28 Mar. '33   --------   --------   --------

35. IN A PERSIAN GARDEN: Myself when young (Omar Khayyam, trans. Fitzgerald-Liza Lehmann) (Or. dir.
by Nathaniel Shilkret)
BS-82332-1,-1A,-2   20 April '34   1706   DA 1318   --------   CAE 158   77.43

*36. A Kingdom by the Sea (Fee-Sommevell) (Pf. Stewart Wille)
CS-74704-1,-2,-3   16 Dec. '32   --------   --------   --------   OASI 5865

37. A Kingdom by the Sea (Fee-Sommevell) (Pf. Stewart Wille)
CS-046068-1,-1A   4 Jan. '40   --------   --------   --------

v

*38. THE KING'S HENCHMAN: Oh, Caesar, great wert thou! (Finale, Act 1) (Edna St. Vincent Millay-Deems Taylor)
(E) (w. Metropolitan Opera Chor. & Orch. dir. by Giulio Setti)
CVE-43613-1,-2,-3   5 April '28   (6845)   -------   -------   76.00
                                    8103

*39. THE KING'S HENCHMAN: Nay, Maccus, lay him down (Finale, Act 3) (Edna St Vincent Millay-Deems Taylor)
(E) (w. Metropolitan Opera Chor. & Orch. dir. by Giulio Setti) (CR)
CVE-43614-1,-2,-3   5 April '28   (6845)   -------   CAL 171   76.00
                                    8103
                                    11-8932

*40. Last Night When We Were Young (E. Y. Harburg-Harold Arlen) (Or. Nathaniel Shilkret)
CS-95370-1,-1A   10 Oct. '35   11877   -------   -------   77.43

41. Life is a Dream (Used in M-G-M film "The Prodigal" - "The Southerner") (Arthur Freed-Oskar Straus)
(Or. Nathaniel Shilkret)
BVE-67493-1,-2   6 Mar. '31   1507   DA 1206   CAE 158   77.43

*42. Love's Old Sweet Song (G. Clifton Bingham-J. L. Molloy) (Pf. Roy Shields)
------- (Test recording) 13 April '25   -------

*43. Love Went A-Riding (Frank Bridge) (Pf. accompaniment)
------- (Test recording) 18 Mar. '25   -------

44. THE MERRY MOUNT: Oh, 'tis an Earth Defiled (Howard Hanson) (w. Metropolitan Opera House Orch.
cond. by Wilfred Pelletier) (CR)
CS-81086-1,-1A,-2,-2A 19 Jan. '34   7959   ED 24   CAL 171   77.43
                                     11-8932

45. MUSIC IN THE AIR: And Love Was Born (Hammerstein II-Kern) (Or. Nathaniel Shilkret)
BS-74656-1,-2   8 Dec. '32   1612   DA 1313   ERAT-24   77.43

46. MUSIC IN THE AIR: The Song Is You (Hammerstein II-Kern)   (Or. Nathaniel Shilkret)
BS-74653-1,-2   8 Dec. '32   1612   DA 1313   -------   77.43

47. My Own United States (Stanislaus Stangé-Julian Edwards, Orch. Reibold) (Or. Pelletier)
BS-036852-1;-1A,-2,-2A 3 May '39   4433   -------   -------   78.26

*48. THE NEW MOON: Lover Come Back To Me (Oscar Hammerstein II-Sigmund Romberg) (Pf. Stewart Wille)
BVE-67495-1   6 Mar. '31   DA 1200   CAE 160   77.43
                                                CAL 168

*49. THE NEW MOON: Wanting You (Oscar Hammerstein II-Sigmund Romberg) (Pf. Stewart Wille)
BVE-67494-1   6 Mar. '31   DA 1200   CAE 217   77.43

50. None But the Lonely Heart (Goethe, trans. Mey-Tchaikovsky, Op. 6, No. 6) (E) (Or. N. Shilkret)
BS-82333-1,-2   20 April '34   DA 1383   CAE 158   77.43
                                                CAL 168
                                                VIC 1340
                                                  CAE 217

51. Oh That We Two Were Maying (Charles Kingsley-Ethelbert Nevin, Op. 2, No. 8) (Or. Bourdon)
BVE-35474-1,-2,-3,-4,-5,-6   24 May '26   DA 829   --------   76.60

*52. Old Black Joe (Stephen C. Foster, arr. Bourdon) (w. Shannon Qt.) (Hp. Lapitino; Or. Bourdon)
BVE-37880-1,-2,-3   31 Mar. '27   DA 909   CAL 168   76.60
                                                CAE 217

*53. On the Road to Mandalay (Rudyard Kipling-Oley Speaks) (E) (Pf. Stewart Wille)
CVE-45190-1   29 May '28   --------   --------

54. On the Road to Mandalay (Rudyard Kipling-Oley Speaks) (E) (Or. N. Shilkret)
CS-95371-1,-1A   10 Oct. '35   DB 3036   CAL 168   77.43
                   11877   CAE 160
                   11-8862

55. OTELLO: Credo in un Dio crudel (Verdi) (I) (Or. Alexander Smallens)
CS-02174-1,-1A   19 Oct. '36   --------   --------

OTELLO: Abridged version in 12 parts (w. Giovanni Martinelli, Helen Jepson, Nicolas Massue, Herman Dreeben, with members of the Metropolitan Opera House Chorus and Orchestra, cond. by Wilfred Pelletier) (Sung in Italian) (Album M-620)

56.[1]. Inaffia l'ugola! (Brindisi) (Tibbett, Massue, Dreeben & Chorus)
CS-036849-1,-1A   3 May '39   DB 5716   VIC 1185   78.26
                   15801   DB 5788   VIC 1365
                   15807
                   15989

No.	Title / Matrix / Takes / Dates				Speed
57.[4].	Vanne! La tua meta...Credo in un Dio crudel (Tibbett)				
	CS-036855-1,-1A 3 May '39	15802	DB 5717	LM 6705-4	78.26
	-2,-2A 9 May '39	15810	DB 5789	VIC 1185	
		15992		VIC 1365	
				ERAT 24	
58.[5].	Non pensateci più... Tu? Indietro!...Ora e per sempre addio (Tibbett, Martinelli)				
	CS-036869-1 9 May '39	15803	DB 5718	VIC 1185	78.26
		15811&15993	DB 5790	VIC 1365	
	-2,-2A 9 May '39	15803		LM 6174-4	78.26
		15811			
		15993			
59.[6].	E qual certezza sognate...Era la notte (Tibbett)				
	CS-036854-1,-1A 3 May '39	15803	DB 5718	VIC 1185	78.26
		15812	DB 5790	VIC 1365	
		15994		LM 21035	
60.[7].	Oh! mostruosa colpa!...Ah! mille vite...Sì, pel ciel (Tibbett, Martinelli)				
	CS-036870-1,-1A,-2,-2A 9 May '39	15804	DB 5719	VIC 1185	78.26
		15807	DB 5791	VIC 1365	
		15994			
61.[8].	Dio! mi potevi scagliar tutti i mali... Cassio è la! (Tibbett, Martinelli)				
	CS-036871-1,-1A 9 May '39	15804	DB 5720	VIC 1185	78.26
		15808	DB 5792	VIC 1365	
		15993			
62.[9].	Vieni; l'aula è deserta...Questo è una ragna (Tibbett, Martinelli, Massue)				
	CS-036851-1,-1A,-2,-2A 3 May '39	15805	DB 5720	VIC 1185	78.26
		15809	DB 5792	VIC 1365	
		15992			
63.	THE PACKET BOAT: Roustabout (Bradley-Hughes) (E) (Pf. Stewart Wille)				
	BVE-45188-1,-2,-3 29 May '28				---
64.	I PAGLIACCI: Sì può?...Sì può? (Prologo, pt. 1) (Leoncavallo) (I) (Or. Bourdon)				
	CVE-35481-1,-2 7 June '26	6587		CAL 171	77.43
				VIC 1340	
				LM 20124	
	-3 7 June '26	6587	DB 975		77.43

65. I PAGLIACCI: Un nido di memorie (Prologo, pt. 2) (Leoncavallo) (I) (Or. Bourdon)
CVE-35482-1,-2,-3   7 June '26   6587   DB 975   --------   CAL 171
                                                                 VIC 1340   77.43
                                                                 LM 20124

66. Pilgrim's Song (Tolstoi, trans. England – Tchaikovsky, Op. 47, No. 5) (E) (Or. N. Shilkret)
CS-74654-1,-2   8 Dec. '32   7779   DB 1945.   --------   VIC 1340   77.43
                                                               LM 20124

*PORGY AND BESS: Selections from the DuBose Heyward-George Gershwin opera (w. Helen Jepson and
the orchestra and chorus of the original New York production, cond. by Alexander Smallens)
(Recorded under the personal supervision of the composer) (Album C-25)

67.[1]. It Ain't Necessarily So (Tibbett & Chorus)
CS-95466-1,-2   23 Oct. '35   11878   DB 2735   ED 44   ERAT 23   77.43
                                          DB 3395   CAL 500
                                                             CAM 6

68.[2]. The Buzzard Song (Tibbett & Chorus)
CS-95389-1,-2,-2A   14 Oct. '35   --------   --------   --------   --------
         -3   23 Oct. '35   11878   DB 2735   CAL 500   77.43
                                                                        CAM 6
                                                                        AVM 1-1742

69.[3]. (a) Summertime & Crap Game (Tibbett & Jepson);   (b) A Woman is a Sometime Thing (Tibbett)
CS-95387-1   23 Oct. '35   11879   DB 2736   --------   CAL 500   77.43
                                                             CAM 6

70.[4]. Bess, You Is My Woman Now (Tibbett & Jepson)
CS-95388-1   14 Oct. '35   11879   DB 2736   --------   CAL 500   77.43
                                      DB 3396   CAM 6
                                                           AVM 1-1742

71.[5]. I Got Plenty o' Nuttin' (Tibbett)
CS-95390-1,-1A   14 Oct. '35   --------   DB 2737   ED 44   CAL 500   77.43
         -2,-3   23 Oct. '35   11880   DB 3395   CAM 6
                                11-8860   AVM 1-1742

72.[6] Where Is My Bess? (Tibbett)
CS-95467-1,-2   23 Oct. '35   11880   DB 2737   --------   CAL 500   77.43
                                                               CAM 6

*73. Retreat (Composer unknown) (Pf. accompaniment)
------- (Test recording) 18 Mar. '25 --------   --------   --------

74. RIGOLETTO: Cortigiani, vil razza, dannata (Verdi) (Or. Alexander Smallens)
CS-02173-1,-2,-3   19 Oct. '36   --------   --------   OASI 5861

75. RIGOLETTO: Sì, vendetta, tremenda vendetta (Verdi) (w. Amelita Galli-Curci) (I) (Or. Bourdon)
BVE-35447-1,-2,-3,-4   7 May '26   --------   --------   --------

76. THE ROGUE SONG: The Narrative (from the M-G-M film) (Clifford Grey-Herbert Stothart)(Or. cond. by N.Shilkret)
BVE-58188-1,-2,-3   13 Jan. '30   1446   DA 1101   CAL 168   76.60

77. THE ROGUE SONG: The Rogue Song (from the M-G-M film) (Clifford Grey, Herbert Stothart)
(Or. cond. by N. Shilkret)
BVE-58187-1,-2,-3   13 Jan. '30   1446   DA 1101   CAE 160   76.60

78. THE ROGUE SONG: When I'm Looking At You (from the M-G-M film) (Clifford Grey-Herbert Stothart)
(Or. cond. by N. Shilkret)
BVE-58195-1,-2,-3,-4   15 Jan. '30   1447   DA 1102   --------   76.60

*79. THE ROGUE SONG: The White Dove (from the M-G-M film) (Clifford Grey - arr. from Franz Lehar
by Herbert Stothart) (Or. cond. by N. Shilkret)
BVE-58196-1,-2,-3   15 Jan. '30   1447   DA 1102   --------   76.60

80. SEMELE: Where'er You Walk (G. F. Handel) (E) (Pf. Stewart Wille)
CS-046065-1,-2,-2A   4 Jan. '40   17456   (DB 5849)   ED 59   LCT 1158
                                                                    LCT 1115   78.26

81. Shake Your Brown Feet, Honey (Langston Hughes-Carpenter) (E) (Pf. Stewart Wille)
BVE-45187-1,-2,-3   29 May '28   --------   --------   --------

82. Short'nin' Bread (Clement Wood-Jacques Wolfe) (Pf. Stewart Wille)
PBVE-68332-1,-2   29 Oct. '31   --------   --------   --------

*83. SHOW BOAT: Ol' Man River (Oscar Hammerstein II - Jerome Kern) (Pf. Stewart Wille)
CS-74705-1,-2   16 Dec. '32   --------   --------   OASI 5864

84. SIMON BOCCANEGRA: Dinne...alcun là non vedesti?...Figlia! tal nome palpito (Verdi) (I)
(w. Rose Bampton & Members of the Metropolitan Opera House Orchestra, cond. by Wilfred Pelletier)
CS-036853-1,-1A   3 May '39   15642   DB 3950   ERAT 24
                                          DB 6018   COLH 127   78.26

85. SIMON BOCCANEGRA: Plebe!.. Patrizi!.. Popolo...Piango su voi, sul placido (Verdi) (I) (w. Rose Bampton, Giovanni Martinelli, Leonard Warren, Robert Nicholson, & Members of the Metropolitan Opera House Chorus and Orchestra, cond. by Wilfred Pelletier)
CS-036850-1,-1A 3 May '39 15642 DB 3950 ------ LM 6171-3 78.26
                                   DB 6018   LCT 6701

86. Song of the Flea (Goethe, trans. Newmarch - Moussorgsky) (E) (Or. Rosario Bourdon)
CVE-34931-1,-2,-3,-4 3 Mar. '26 ------ ------ ------

*87. Song of the Flea (Goethe, trans. Newmarch - Moussorgsky) (E) (Or. N. Shilkret)
CS-74655-1 8 Dec. '32 7779 ------ VIC 1340 77.43
                                     CAL 168   77.43
      -2   8 Dec. '32 7779 DB 1945 ------

88. Song of the Flea (Goethe, trans. Newmarch - Moussorgsky) (E) (Pf. Stewart Wille)
CS-75707-1,-2 28 Mar. '33 ------ ------ ------

89. TALES OF HOFFMANN: Barcarolle ("Belle nuit, o nuit d'amour") (Offenbach) (E) (w. Lucrezia Bori)
(Harp: Lapitino; Or. Bourdon)
BVE-38855-1,-2,-3 1 June '27 3043 DA 912 ------ 77.43
                               1747

90. TANNHÄUSER: Wie Todesahnung Dämmrung deckt die Lande...0 du, mein holder Abendstern (Wagner) (G)
(Or. N. Shilkret)
CS-82330-1,-1A 20 April '34 8452 DB 2262 ------ CAL 171 77.43
                              11-8862   LM 20135

91. THEODORA: Defend Her! Heaven (G. F. Handel) (E) (Pf. Stewart Wille)
CS-046066-1,-2,-3,-3A 4 Jan. '40 17456 (DB5849) ED 59 ------ 78.26

92. Thy Beaming Eyes (W. H. Gardner-Edward A. MacDowell) (Or. Bourdon)
BVE-35475-1,-2,-3,-4 24 May '26 1172 DA 829 ------ CAL 168 77.43
      -5,-6,-7,-8   7 June '26

93. TOSCA: Tre sbirri, una carrozza, presto (Te Deum) (Puccini) (I) (w. Metropolitan Opera House Chor. and Orch., cond. by Giulio Setti)
CVE-51116-1,-2,-3 3 April '29 8124 DB 1298 ------ VIC 1340 76.00
      -4   10 April '29 8124   CAL 171   76.00
                                11-8861

*94. Travelin' to de Grave (Spiritual, arr. Reddick) (E) (Pf. Stewart Wille)
BVE-45189-1,-2,-3 29 May '28 ------ ------ ------

95. Uncle Ned (Stephen C. Foster, arr. Bourdon) (w. Shannon Qt.) (Or. Bourdon)
BVE-37881-1,-2,-3,-4   31 Mar. '27   --------   --------   --------   77.43
-5,-6,-7   31 May '27   1265   DA 909

DIE WALKÜRE: Wotan's Farewell (Wagner) (G) (w. Philadelphia Symphony Orch., cond by Leopold Stokowski)
(included in Album M-248, "Excerpts from Act III", arr. Stokowski)

96.[4]. Leb' wohl du kühnes, herrliches Kind!
CS-83105-1,-1A   30 April '34   8543   DB 2471   --------   77.43
8549   DB 7958
16643

97.[5]. Denn Einer nur freie die Braut...Der Augen leuchtendes Paar
CS-83106-1,-1A   30 April '34   8544   DB 2472   --------   77.43
8546   DB 7958
16643

98.[6]. Zum letzten Mal letz' es mich heut' mit des Lebeswohles
CS-83107-1,-1A   30 April '34   8544   DB 2472   --------   77.43
8547   DB 7957
16642

99.[7]. Loge hör'! Lausche hieher!
CS-83108-1,-1A   30 April '34   8545   DB 2473   --------   77.43
8548   DB 7956
16641

100.[8]. Wer meines Speeres Spitze fürchtet
CS-83109-1,-1A   30 April '34   8545   DB 2473   --------   77.43
8549   DB 7955
16640

101. Der Wanderer (Schmidt von Lübeck-Schubert, D. 439) (E) (Pf. Stewart Wille)
CS-046069-1,-1A   4 Jan. '40   15891   (DB 5762)   VIC 1340   78.26

102. Without a Song (from "Great Day"; used in the M-G-M film "The Prodigal" - "The Southerner")
(Rose Eliscu-Vincent Youmans) (Or. N. Shilkret)
BVE-67492-1,-2   6 Mar. '31   1507   DA 1206   CAE 158   77.43

N O T E S

2.   "Recorded at the request of The Gramophone Co."

4.   Take 2 issued on post-war pressings only.

5.   Take 1 issued on post-war pressings only.

10.   Take 4 issued on post-war pressings only.

13/19.   The "Trinity Choir" was the name given to the Victor "house" chorus when singing religious music. On this occasion it was made up as follows:
         Sopranos: L. I. Marsh, O. Kline, D. Baker, R. Rogers, E. S. Hager
         Altos: E. Baker, H. Clark, R. Bryant, E. Indemauer
         Basses: F. Croxton, W. Glenn, E. Shaw, J. Stanley, S. Baughman

20.   Recorded in Hollywood. Pre-war issues only.

21.   Sung ½ tone lower than No. 20. BVE-69068-3 is a solo. It was played during the recording of BVE-69071-2, at which time Tibbett added the tenor part to the refrain. This dual recording was issued only in post-war editions.

22.   Both pre- and post-war pressings of 1550 used this same recording.

24.   A second trial session for Victor (see note under 43.) took place on 13 April '25. Both electrical and acoustical recordings were made that day and it is the author's assumption that these were electrical recordings. Like other tests, they bear no numbers. (See also notes under 30. and 42.)

26.   Take 2 was made in Hollywood and issued on post-war pressings only. Note words: "...and why so sad gang ye?" Take 4 was made in Camden, N.J. and issued on pre-war pressings. Note: "...and why so sad go ye?"

29.   Post-war pressings are of the same performance, either re-cut masters or possibly Take 1A.

30.   See note under 24.

32.   Post-war pressings were from re-cut master with finer grooves, thus leaving a larger center, but the performance is the same.

34.   Marked "Personal Recording".

36.   Marked "Personal Recording".

38.   Tibbett created the role of Eadgar at the Metropolitan Opera House world premiere on 17 February 1927. The music here recorded from Act 1 is sung in the opera by Maccus, a minor role, created by William Gustafson.

xiii

39. The music here recorded is from the role Tibbett created.

40. This song was composed for the United Artists film, "Metropolitan", but for some reason was not used in the final release.

42. See note under 24.

43. This selection (and also No. 73) were Tibbett's "trial" or audition recordings for Victor. Although a few experimental electrical recordings had been made in February, 1925, and one studio was used for electrical recording from March 11 onwards, the two Tibbett tests were probably acoustical recordings.

48/49. These recordings were made as "Personal Recordings" for the artist, so their public release was not anticipated. This probably explains why they were made with piano accompaniment. Why they were not remade with orchestra is not known.

52. On this occasion the "Shannon Quartet" consisted of Lewis James, Charles Harrison, James Shaw and Wilfred Glenn.

53. Marked "Personal Recording".

67/72. The New York premiere of <u>Porgy & Bess</u> took place on 10 October, 1935. It is interesting to note that the first session of this recording series took place (in Liederkranz Hall, N.Y.) just four days later. Plans for the recording session, using two prominent Metropolitan Opera artists, must have been made well in advance of the New York opening!

73. See note under 43.

79. The music, originally from Lehar's "Zigeunerliebe" was recorded by John McCormack with only slightly altered words as "Balalaika: The Magic of Your Love".

83. Marked "Personal Recording".

87. Take 1 issued on post-war pressings only.

93. Take 4 issued on post-war pressings only.

94. In this recording the "Shannon Quartet" consisted of Charles Hart, Lambert Murphy, Royal Dadmun and James Stanley. There is a note in the recording book: "Date delayed due to absence of Crooks, replaced by Hart"., but Crooks was present, along with Murphy, Dadman and Baughman in Camden the next day to record with Louise Homer and Mark Andrews (organ) while Bori and Tibbett were recording at Liederkranz Hall in New York.

II. OTHER RECORDINGS

Lawrence Tibbett's career began just before the advent of electrical recording (see NOTE No. 39), covered the early days of American Radio and the introduction of the sound motion picture; he was very active in all these fields. Instantaneous recording from radio became more or less common by 1934, when there were a number of commercial studios established which would make "custom recordings" for artists. Initially, such recordings were cut on aluminum; later superior recordings were cut on acetate-coated aluminum discs. Many such discs have survived from programs such as "The Packard Hour", the "General Motors Hour", "The Atwater Kent Hour", "The Ford Sunday Evening Hour" and "The Telephone Hour", and many of these have appeared, unfortunately often unidentified as to date and source, on "Private Label" Lps. In addition, Tibbett took part in some 34 Saturday Afternoon Metropolitan Opera Broadcasts from 1932 through 1950; most of these performances have been preserved. Tibbett was one of the first artists of international reputation to appear in full-length motion pictures. These sound tracks have been made available through television runs to thousands with today's tape recorders. In addition, from time to time, pressings of recordings made for use in some of these films have turned up. This great mass of radio and motion picture material exists in private collections, with much of it widely available on "private" Lp issues. The listings which follow undoubtedly represent only a sampling of such "non-commercial" recordings by Lawrence Tibbett.

1.) METROPOLITAN OPERA BROADCASTS

CONTES D'HOFFMAN (Tibbett as Lindorf, Coppelius, Dapertutto & Dr. Miracle) (w. Bovy; Maison, &c., cond. de Abravanel) 23 Jan.'37 (UORC 206) (Highlights, HduC)
EMPEROR JONES (Brutus Jones) (World Premier) (cond. Serafin) 7 Jan.'33
FAUST (Valentin) (w. Norena, Martinelli, Pinza, cond. Hasselmans) 17 Feb.'34
FORZA DEL DESTINO (Don Carlos) (w. Roman, Jagel, Pinza, cond. Walter) 23 Jan.'43 (EJS 211)
FORZA DEL DESTINO (Don Carlos) (w. Roman, Jagel, Pinza, cond. Walter) 27 Nov.'43 (EJS 561?,inc.)
KHOVANCHINA (Ivan) (w. Stevens, Stoska, Kullman, Hines, Weede, cond. Cooper) 25 Feb.'50 (EJS 262, inc.; UORC 295)
MERRY MOUNT (Wrestling Bradford) (w. Ljungberg, Swarthout, Johnson, cond. Serafin) 10 Feb.'34 (World Premier) (EJS 134)
OTELLO (Iago) (w. Rethberg, Martinelli, cond. Panizza) 12 Feb.'38 (EJS 181)
OTELLO (Iago) (w. Caniglia, Martinelli, cond. Panizza) 3 Dec.'38 (EJS 281)
OTELLO (Iago) (w. Rethberg, Martinelli, cond. Panizza) 24 Feb.'40 (EJS 106)
OTELLO (Iago) (w. Roman, Martinelli, cond. Panizza) 18 Jan.'41 (UORC 192) (EJS 260)
PAGLIACCI (Tonio) (w. Q. Mario, Martinelli, cond. Bellezza) 10 Mar.'34 (EJS 105)
PAGLIACCI (Tonio) (w. Greco, Martinelli, cond. Calusio) 1 Feb.'41 (EJS 105)
PELLEAS ET MELISANDE (Golaud) (w. Sayão, Singher, Kipnis, cond. Cooper) 13 Jan.'45 (UORC 187)
PETER GRIMES (Capt. Balstrode) (w. Stoska, Madeira, Hines, cond. Cooper) 12 Feb.'49

PETER IBBETSON (Col. Ibbetson) (w. Bori, Swarthout, Johnson, cond. Serafin) 26 Mar. '32 (inc.)
PETER IBBETSON (Col. Ibbetson) (w. Bori, Swarthout, Johnson, cond. Serafin) 17 Mar. '34 (UORC 143)
RIGOLETTO (Rigoletto) (w. Pons, Jagel, cond. Panizza) 28 Dec. '35 (Highlights, EJS 551 & 213)
RIGOLETTO (Rigoletto) (w. Pons, Kiepura, cond. Papi) 11 Mar. '39 (EJS 131)
SIMON BOCCANEGRA (Doge) (w. Müller, Martinelli, Pinza, cond. Serafin) (First U.S. prod.) 28 Jan. '31 (inc.)
SIMON BOCCANEGRA (Doge) (w. Rethberg, Martinelli, Pinza, cond. Panizza) 16 Feb. '35 (UORC 161 + EJS 177)
SIMON BOCCANEGRA (Doge) (w. Rethberg, Martinelli, Pinza, cond. Panizza) 21 Jan. '39 (EJS 108)
IL TABARRO (Michele) (w. Albanese, Jagel, cond. Sodero) 5 Jan. '46 (EJS 193)
TANNHÄUSER (Wolfram) (w. Rethberg, Melchior, cond. Bodanzky) 16 Apr. '32 (inc.)
TANNHÄUSER (Wolfram) (w. Flagstad, Melchior, List, cond. Bodanzky) 18 Jan. '36 (EJS 109)
TOSCA (Scarpia) (w. Moore, Peerce, cond. Sodero) 9 Feb. '46 (Met. Arch.) (Pvt. tape)
TOSCA (Scarpia) (w. Dosia, Peerce, cond. Antonicelli) 20 Nov. '47
TRAVIATA (Germont) (w. Bori, Tokatyan, cond. Serafin) 28 Jan. '33
TRAVIATA (Germont) (w. Ponselle, Jagel, cond. Panizza) 12 Dec. '35 (EJS 107)
TRAVIATA (Germont) (w. Jepson, Crooks, cond. Panizza) 23 Dec. '39 (Highlights, EJS 540)
TRAVIATA (Germont) (w. Novotna, Peerce, cond. Panizza) 29 Nov. '41
TRAVIATA (Germont) (w. Albanese, Kullmann, cond. Sodero) 5 Dec. '42
TRAVIATA (Germont) (w. Albanese, Peerce, cond. Sodero) 1 Jan. '44
TRAVIATA (Germont) (w. Albanese, Peerce, cond. Sodero) 17 Feb. '45 (AFRS No. 12)

2.) COVENT GARDEN OPERA BROADCASTS

DON JUAN DE MANARA (Don Juan) (w. Andreva, Noble, Williams, cond. Goossens) 28 June '37 (Met. Arch.)

3.) MOTION PICTURE SOUND TRACK MATERIAL

When Tibbett made the film "Metropolitan", recording for the film was cut on 12" inside-out 78 rpm discs. Even though contemporary reviews in the New York Times indicate that the film was released by Twentieth Century-Fox, the labels on the records show United Artists Corp. as the source. No complete listing of these discs has been found, but occasionally copies turn up in private collections, i.e.:

Wax No. 1378-2   CARMEN: Votre toast (Tibbett, w. Chorus & Orch.)
        1378-10   PAGLIACCI: Vesti la giubba (Tibbett & Orch.)
        1378-11   CARMEN: Je dis que rien (first half only) (Carroll Weiskopf & Orch.)
        1378-20   BARBIERE DI SIVIGLIA: Largo al factotum (Tibbett & Orch.)
        1378-25   De Glory Road: several alternate endings (Tibbett & piano)
        1378-41   Last night when we were young (Tibbett & Carroll Weiskopf w. Orch.)

"The New Moon" (Hammerstein II - Romberg). This 1930 film, with Grace Moore, has been shown on U.S. television under the title "Parisian Belle", and about 30 minutes of the sound track has been issued on an Lp disc labeled BMPM 1919.

Under Your Spell (Arthur Schwartz): The title song from the Tibbett film of this name has been issued on an Lp labeled JJA 19757: Arthur Schwartz, Vol. II, 1933-1937. The song "Amigo" for this same film has been issued on ROCOCO No. 5324. The entire sound track is known to be on private tape.

4. RADIO AND LATE STUDIO RECORDINGS. Note: The producers of Lp recordings for "private" circulation are notably lax in providing information about the sources of their material. Some of the EJS recordings were made from radio transcriptions from Mr. Tibbett's collection, and with his permission. Sources and dates are for the most part suggested and are based on considerable research from published radio programs. However, dates given are to be taken as probable or possible, and are subject to correction.

Accentuate the Positive	"Lucky Strike Hit Parade"	25 Feb. '46	Pvt. Tape
Accentuate the Positive	"Lucky Strike Hit Parade"	date?	EMP 804
Adeste Fideles (spoken intro. by Tibbett, Organ: Len Salvo)(Salvation Army)		Nov. '49	A.O.S.
Amigo (from film "Under Your Spell")	(from sound track?)		R.5324
Amor Amor (Pirandelli)	"Packard Hour"?	? '37	EJS 397
ANDREA CHENIER: Nemico della patria?	"Packard Hour"?	1935-36	EJS 110
ANDREA CHENIER: Nemico della patria? (w. dubbed orchestra) (R 5226?)		ca. 1955	SC 886
Because (d'Hardelot)	Studio recording	ca. 1955	H.50266
			AR 18171
Begin the Beguine (Porter)	Studio recording	ca. 1955	H.50266
CARMEN: Votre toast	"Packard Hour"	18 Sept. '34/	
		14 Jan. '36	EJS 397
CONTES D'HOFFMANN: Je me nomme Coppelius	Met. broadcast?	?23 Jan. '37	EJS 181
CONTES D'HOFFMANN: Scintille, diamant	"Packard Hour" (R 5266?)	ca. 1934	EJS 110
CONTES D'HOFFMANN: Scintille, diamant	(w. Pf. accompaniment)	? '36	EJS 295
CUBAN LOVE SONG: Cuban love song (w. Pf.)	Victor Discography #20	28 Oct. '31	EMP 804
CUBAN LOVE SONG: Tramps at Sea (w. Pf.)	Victor Discography #23	26 Oct. '31	EMP 804
Danny Deever (Kipling-Damrosch)	Studio recording	ca. 1955	H.50266
			AR 18171
Deep River (Spiritual)	Studio recording	ca. 1955	AR 1627
			AR 18171
			H.50266
DESERT SONG: One Alone	"Lucky Strike Hit Parade"	ca. 1946	EMP 804
DON GIOVANNI: Finch' han del vino	Studio recording (w. dubbed orch.)	ca. 1955	AR 1627
			AR 1588
			AR 1904
DON GIOVANNI: Madamina, il catalogo	Studio recording (w. dubbed orch.)	ca. 1955	EJS 181
			SC 886

Title	Note	Date	Catalog
Don't fence me in	"Lucky Strike Hit Parade	?ca. 1946	EMP 804
Drink to me only with thine eyes	"Ford Sunday Evening Hour"	?ca. 1947	R.5324
EMPEROR JONES: Condensed version	"Packard Hour"	16 Oct. '34	EJS 124
EMPEROR JONES: Scenes	Film sound track?	?ca. 1936	R.5324
FALSTAFF: È sogno o realtà?	Victor Discography # 28	3 Mar. '26	Pvt. Tape
FALSTAFF: È sogno o realtà?	"Packard Hour"	20 Feb. '35	EJS 110
FALSTAFF: È sogno o realtà?	Studio recording (w. dubbed orch.)	ca. 1955	SC 886
			AR 1627
			R.5266
	*TAP recording mislabeled "Quand'ero paggio"		TAP 319*
FALSTAFF: Quand'ero paggio	Studio recording (w. dubbed orch.)	ca. 1955	SC 886
FALSTAFF: L'Onore! Ladri!			TAP 314
	Studio recording (w. dubbed orch.)	ca. 1955	SC 866
			AR 1627
FAUST: Act 2, Sc. 1, incl."Le Veau d'Or"	"Packard Hour"	?4 Feb. '36	R. 5324
			EJS 124
FAUST: Vous qui faites l'endormie	"Packard Hour"	?4 Feb. '36	R.5266
			EJS 110
FAUST: Death of Valentin (in English)	Radio	? '47	UORC 151
FORZA DEL DESTINO: Urna fatale	"Telephone Hour"	? '43	Pvt. Tape
De Glory Road	"Packard Hour"?	18 Sept. '34/	
		5 Nov. '35, or	
		17 Mar. '36	
De Glory Road	Studio recording	ca. 1955	EJS 397
			H.50266
			AR 1627
Hallelujah Rhythm	Possibly Victor Discography # 33	?19 Oct. '36	AR 18171
HERODIADE: Vision fugitive	"Packard Hour"	29 Oct. '35/	EJS 397
HERODIADE: Vision fugitive	Studio recording (w. dubbed orch.)	11 Feb. 36	EJS 110
			R.5266
			SC 886
Home on the Range	Studio recording	ca. 1955	AR 18171
			H.50266
I dream of Jeannie with the light brown hair	Radio	ca. 1947	R.5324
In the Gloaming (Harrison)	"Telephone Hour"	? '43	Pvt. Tape
Johnny the One (Saks)	"Telephone Hour"	? '43	Pvt. Tape
THE KING'S HENCHMAN: Finale, Act 3 (w. Deems Taylor)	"Packard Hour"	20 Nov. '34	EJS 124
Life is a dream	Victor Discography # 41	6 Mar. '31	EMP 804
MARTHA: Porter Song (in English)	"Packard Hour"	18 Dec. '34	R.5266
			EJS 110

Title	Source	Date	Issue
MEISTERSINGER: Was duftet doch der Flieder (in English, mislabeled)	"Packard Hour"	2 Oct. '34	EJS 110
MEISTERSINGER: Was duftet doch der Flieder (in German)	Studio recording (w. dubbed orch.)	ca. 1955	R.5266 / SC 886
Minnelied (Brahms) (in English)	"Packard Hour"	27 Nov. '34	EJS 397
NEW MOON: Lover come back to me	Victor Discography # 48	6 Mar. '31	EMP 804
NEW MOON: Wanting You	Victor Discography # 49	6 Mar. '31	EMP 804
Noel (A Catholic tale I have to tell)	Private recording	? '36	UORC 197 / EJS 295
On the Road to Mandalay	"Packard Hour"	5 Mar. '35/ 12 Nov. '35	EJS 397
On the Road to Mandalay	Victor Discography # 53	29 May '28	EMP 804
On the Road to Mandalay	Studio recording	ca. 1955	AR 18171 / H.50266
OTELLO: Credo in un Dio crudel	Radio ?	?	R.5266
PAGLIACCI: Prologo	"Packard Hour"	25 Sept. '34/26 Nov. '35/ 31 Dec. '35 or 17 Mar. '36	EJS 397 / EJS 397
PAGLIACCI: Vesti la giubba (w/o recit.)	"Packard Hour"	25 Sept. '34	R.5324
PAGLIACCI: Recitar...Vesti la giubba	?	21 Jan. '36	EJS 124
PORGY & BESS: I got plenty o' nuttin'	Studio recording	ca. 1955	AR 1627
PORGY & BESS: It ain't necessarily so	Studio recording	ca. 1955	AR 1627
RIGOLETTO: Cortigiani, vil razza	"Packard Hour"	5 Nov. '35/ 7 Jan. '36	EJS 397
RIGOLETTO: Pari siamo	Studio recording (w. dubbed orch.)	ca. 1955	SC 886
ROGUE SONG: The Rogue Song	Victor Discography # 77	13 Jan. '30	EMP 804
ROGUE SONG: The Rogue Song, with spoken intro. by Tibbett	Radio	ca. 1947	R.5324
ROGUE SONG: The White Dove	Victor Discography # 79	15 Jan. '30	EMP 804
ROMEO ET JULIETTE: Ballad of Queen Mab	"Packard Hour"	10 Mar. '36	R.5266 / EJS 110
SHOW BOAT: Ol' Man River	Studio recording	ca. 1955	H.50266 / AR 1627
SIMON BOCCANEGRA: Tibbett discusses	Metropolitan Opera Intermission	2 Apr. '60	Pvt. Tape / AR 18171
Song of the Flea	Studio recording	ca. 1955	H.50266

Suomi (Song of Finland, arr. by Frank Black) Sung by Kirsten Flagstad, Karin Branzell, Lauritz Melchior and Lawrence Tibbett. Finnish war relief program, 27 Dec. '39. Orch. dir by Eugene Goossens. 78 rpm "Melotone" pressings (not numbered) sold for charitable purposes. rr. on EJS 322

Title / Aria	Source	Date	Label
TABARRO: Scorre fiume	"Packard Hour"	30 Oct. '34/20 Mar. '35 or 12 Nov. '35	EJS 110
TABARRO: Scorre fiume	Studio recording (w. dubbed orch.)	ca. 1955	R.5266
Through the Years	Radio, "Voice of Firestone"?	ca. 1950	R.5324
Tommy Lad (Margetson)	Radio, "Voice of Firestone"?	ca. 1950	R.5324
TOSCA: Gia mi dicon venal	"Packard Hour"	25 Feb. '36	R.5266
TOSCA: Excerpts from Act II (w. G. Moore) Cincinnati		'45	EJS 110
TRAVIATA: Di Provenza	"Packard Hour"	27 Nov. '34/22 Oct. '35	EJS 456
TRAVIATA: Di Provenza	Radio?	17 Dec. '35 or 18 Feb. '36	EJS 110
TROVATORE: Il balen	"Packard Hour"	?	R.5266
		25 Feb. '36	R.5266 EJS 110
The Volga Boatman	Studio recording	ca. 1955	AR 18171 H.50266
Without a Song	Victor Discography # 102	6 Mar. '31	EMP 804
Without a Song	Studio recording	ca. 1955	H.50266
XERXES: Ombra mai fu	"Packard Hour"	19 Nov. '35	EJS 110

NOTE: In the opinion of the compiler of this discography all "ca. 1955" recordings should be avoided. These are not representative of the art of Lawrence Tibbett, and their existence does his memory a great disservice.

KEY TO Lp LABELS

AFRS	Armed Forces Radio Services (16" 33 1/3 rpm discs)
AOS	Army of Stars: Salvation Army Christmas Programs (16" 33 1/3 rpm discs)
AR	Allegro-Royale
EJS	"The Golden Age of Opera" (Private issue Lp discs)
EMP	Empire
H	Halo (also Allegro-Royale issues)
HduC	Histoire du Chant de l'Age d'Or Français, 1930-40
"inc."	Incomplete recording
Met. Arch.	Metropolitan Opera Company Archives
OASI	Private issue Lp - 3 discs: "A Tribute to Tibbett" (all from Victor)
Pvt. Tape	Known to exist in private tape collections
R	Rococo
SC	Scala/Everest
TAP	Top Artist Platters
UORC	"Unique Opera Record Co.", a private label

5.) <u>FILM CREDITS</u>

1930 - THE ROGUE SONG - with Lawrence Tibbett, Catherine Dale Owen, Nance
O'Neil, Judith Vosselli, Ullrich Haupt, Elsa Alsen, Florence Lake,
Lionel Belmore, Wallace MacDonald, Kate Price, H. A. Morgan, Burr
MacIntosh, James Bradbury Jr., Stanley Laurel and Oliver Hardy.
Based on the operetta "Gypsy Love", by Franz Lehar, A. M. Willner
and Robert Bodansky; directed by Lionel Barrymore. A Metro-Goldwyn-
Mayer production.

1930 - NEW MOON - with Lawrence Tibbett, Grace Moore, Adolphe Menjou, Roland
Young, Gus Shy and Emily Fitzroy. An operetta based on "The New Moon"
with music by Sigmund Romberg and the book and lyrics by Oscar Hammerstein II, Frank Mandel and Lawrence Schwab. A Metro-Goldwyn-Mayer
production.

1931 - THE PRODIGAL (also released under the title THE SOUTHERNER) - based
on a story by Bess Meredyth and Wells Root; directed by Harry Pollard.
A Metro-Goldwyn-Mayer production.

> Jeffry Farraday.........Lawrence Tibbett
> Antonia.................Esther Ralston
> Doc.....................Roland Young
> Snipe...................Cliff Edwards
> Rodman Farraday.........Purnell B. Pratt
> Christine...............Hedda Hopper
> Mrs. Farraday...........Emma Dunn
> Hokey...................Stepin Fetchit
> George..................Louis John Bartels
> Carter Jerome...........Theodore Von Eltz
> Peter...................Wally Albright Jr.
> Elsbeth.................Suzanne Ransom
> Naomi...................Gertrude Howard
> Jackson.................John Larkin

1931 - THE CUBAN LOVE SONG - from a story by G. Gardiner Sullivan and
Bess Meredyth; directed by W. S. Van Dyke. A Metro-Goldwyn-Mayer
production.

> Terry Burke.............Lawrence Tibbett
> Nenita..................Lupe Velez
> Romance.................Ernest Torrence
> O. O. Jones.............James Durante
> Crystal.................Karen Morley
> Elvira..................Louise Fazenda
> John....................Hale Hamilton
> Aunt Rosa...............Mathilda Comont
> Terry Jr. ....Phillip Cooper

1935 - METROPOLITAN - based on a story by Bess Meredyth; screenplay by
       Bess Meredyth and George Marlon Jr.; directed by Richard Boleslawski
       and produced by Darryl F. Zanuck for Twentieth Century-Fox.

                    Thomas Renwick.............Lawrence Tibbett
                    Anne Merrill...............Virginia Bruce
                    Ghita Galin................Alice Brady
                    Niki Baroni................Cesar Romero
                    T. Simon Hunter............Thurston Hall
                    Ugo Pizzi..................Luis Alberini
                    Perontelli.................George Marion Sr.
                    Mr. Tolentino..............Adrian Rosley
                    Weidel.....................Christian Rub
                    Marina.....................Ruth Donnelly
                    Marco......................Franklyn Ardell
                    Nello......................Etienne Girardot
                    Charwoman..................Jessie Ralph

1936 - UNDER YOUR SPELL - based on stories by Bernice Mason and Sy Bartlett;
       screenplay by Frances Hyland and Saul Elkins; music and lyrics by
       Arthur Schwartz and Howard Dietz; directed by Otto Ludwig Preminger
       and produced by Twentieth Century-Fox.

                    Anthony Allen..............Lawrence Tibbett
                    Cynthia Drexel.............Wendy Barrie
                    Petroff....................Gregory Ratoff
                    Botts......................Arthur Treacher
                    Count Raul de Rienne.......Gregory Gaye
                    Judge......................Berton Churchill
                    Mr. Twerp..................Jed Prouty
                    Mrs. Twerp.................Claudia Coleman
                    Uncle Bob..................Charles Richman

ACKNOWLEDGEMENTS

Thanks are due to the Stanford Archive of Recorded Sound
"Victor Project" and especially to Mr. Ted Fagan. Assistance with the Victor material was also provided by Darrell
G. Strong. Mr. William Collins has done much research in
an attempt to date radio excerpts. Dr. Thomas R. Bullard
has also helped with the re-issues on Lp.

Opera Biographies

An Arno Press Collection

Albani, Emma. **Forty Years of Song.** With a Discography by W. R. Moran. [1911]

Biancolli, Louis. **The Flagstad Manuscript.** 1952

Bispham, David. **A Quaker Singer's Recollections.** 1921

Callas, Evangelia and Lawrence Blochman. **My Daughter Maria Callas.** 1960

Calvé, Emma. **My Life.** With a Discography by W. R. Moran. 1922

Corsi, Mario. **Tamagno, Il Più Grande Fenomeno Canoro Dell'Ottocento.** With a Discography by W. R. Moran. 1937

Cushing, Mary Watkins. **The Rainbow Bridge.** With a Discography by W. R. Moran. 1954

Eames, Emma. **Some Memories and Reflections.** With a Discography by W. R. Moran. 1927

Gaisberg, F[rederick] W[illiam]. **The Music Goes Round.** 1942

Gigli, Beniamino. **The Memoirs of Beniamino Gigli.** 1957

Hauk, Minnie. **Memories of a Singer.** 1925

Henschel, Horst and Ehrhard Friedrich. **Elisabeth Rethberg:** Ihr Leben und Künstlertum. 1928

Hernandez Girbal, F. **Julian Gayarre:** El Tenor de la Voz de Angel. 1955

Heylbut, Rose and Aimé Gerber. **Backstage at the Metropolitan Opera** (Originally published as **Backstage at the Opera**). 1937

Jeritza, Maria. **Sunlight and Song:** A Singer's Life. 1929

Klein, Herman. **The Reign of Patti.** With a Discography by W. R. Moran. 1920

Lawton, Mary. **Schumann-Heink:** The Last of the Titans. With a Discography by W. R. Moran. 1928

Lehmann, Lilli. **My Path Through Life.** 1914

Litvinne, Félia. **Ma Vie et Mon Art:** Souvenirs. 1933

Marchesi, Blanche. **Singer's Pilgrimage.** With a Discography by W. R. Moran. 1923

Martens, Frederick H. **The Art of the Prima Donna and Concert Singer.** 1923

Maude, [Jenny Maria Catherine Goldschmidt]. **The Life of Jenny Lind.** 1926

Maurel, Victor. **Dix Ans de Carrière, 1887-1897.** 1897

Mingotti, Antonio. **Maria Cebotari,** Das Leben Einer Sangerin. [1950]

Moore, Edward C. **Forty Years of Opera in Chicago.** 1930

Moore, Grace. **You're Only Human Once.** 1944

Moses, Montrose J. **The Life of Heinrich Conried.** 1916

Palmegiani, Francesco. **Mattia Battistini:** Il Re Dei Baritoni. With a Discography by W. R. Moran. [1949]

Pearse, [Cecilia Maria de Candia] and Frank Hird. **The Romance of a Great Singer.** A Memoir of Mario. 1910

Pinza, Ezio and Robert Magidoff. **Ezio Pinza:** An Autobiography. 1946

Rogers, Francis. **Some Famous Singers of the 19th Century.** 1914

Rosenthal, Harold [D.] **Great Singers of Today.** 1966

Ruffo, Titta. **La Mia Parabola:** Memorie. With a Discography by W. R. Moran. 1937

Santley, Charles. **Reminiscences of My Life.** With a Discography by W. R. Moran. 1909

Slezak, Leo. **Song of Motley:** Being the Reminiscences of a Hungry Tenor. 1938

Stagno Bellincioni, Bianca. **Roberto Stagno e Gemma Bellincioni Intimi** *and* Bellincioni, Gemma, **Io e il Palcoscenico:** Trenta e un anno di vita artistica. With a Discography by W. R. Moran. 1943/1920. Two vols. in one.

Tetrazzini, [Luisa]. **My Life of Song.** 1921

Teyte, Maggie. **Star on the Door.** 1958

Tibbett, Lawrence. **The Glory Road.** With a Discography by W. R. Moran. 1933

Traubel, Helen and Richard G. Hubler. **St. Louis Woman.** 1959

Van Vechten, Carl. **Interpreters.** 1920

Wagner, Charles L. **Seeing Stars.** 1940